FRIAR TUCK'S WORD OF THE DAY

VOLUME V

LIVING BEYOND YOUR MEANS

RON BOWELL

Friar Tuck's Word of the Day - Volume Five Living Beyond Your Means

Published by:

Friar Tuck Publishing
1125 West South Street
Salina, Kansas 67401
785-823-0101

Library of Congress Control Number: 2017957475 ISBN:
978-0-9898600-4-8

Printed by Mennonite Press, Inc.

Printed in USA

INTRODUCTION

"Friar Tuck's Word of the Day - Volume V" is the final step in a five year journey… a journey that was undertaken with the heartfelt conviction that spending some quality time in God's word each day can dramatically change a life. When we consent to a daily immersion in the deep waters of Scripture, there is no way we can remain unchanged.

With the Bible, God has given us His wisdom for the ages. He has shown us His plan, and He has introduced us to His Son Jesus, the Savior of the world. Very few of us could sit and read the entire Bible in one sitting, but if we are diligent and disciplined, we can complete this task over time.

The five volumes in the "Friar Tuck's Word of the Day" series of daily devotionals do not cover every verse in the Bible, but they will certainly point you in that direction. Volume III covers every verse in the book of Psalms. Volume IV leads you through every verse in the Gospel of

Luke. And now, Volume V will take you through every verse in the book of Acts over the course of a year.

The book of Acts is a pivotal book in Scripture. The early church had to carry on without Jesus, who had ascended into heaven. But their greatest asset was that they had been filled with His presence through the Holy Spirit of God -- and with the Spirit's help, they were able to "Live Beyond Their Means", as the few became many.

Those early disciples literally changed the world as they laid down their lives for the gospel. Enjoy their stories in Volume V. Better yet, if you will engage with the risen Christ yourself, His Holy Spirit can change your own world today.

It is my hope and prayer that through God's gracious mercy, the words on these pages can affect your life in a way that brings glory to God.

Ron Bowell
Friar Tuck

BASIC INSTRUCTIONS

You will need a printed bible or a computer bible in your favorite version to fully benefit from this devotional. It contains only scripture references (no printed scripture). This is beneficial because your bible is like a letter from God. Become familiar with its pages – its chapters and verses. Treat it as a friend. Use it as a tool. Write in it this year. Make notes on its pages about what God said to you and date them. This will be a source of strength in years to come. If you cannot find a particular book of the bible, almost every bible has an index in the front with a page number where the book can be located. In some of the daily offerings the scripture reference is abbreviated to save space. These are standard abbreviations, but if you have difficulty figuring out what book of Scripture is being referred to, ask your pastor or another seasoned student of the bible for help. Do not hesitate to discuss the daily devotionals with other Christians. Spiritual growth can be boosted and accelerated when we process new information with other believers.

ACKNOWLEDGMENTS

Thanks to the Father for sending us His Son. Thanks to the Lord Jesus Christ for His sacrifice, His healing, and His love. Thanks to the Holy Spirit for coming in fullness, and for helping us understand the truth of Scripture. With God's Spirit, we really can "live beyond our means".

Thanks to June Ferguson for her patient and thorough proof-reading. Thanks to CrossRoads Church for allowing me to be their pastor for all these years. Thanks to those from whom I am still learning on a daily basis. You have modeled the life of Christ for me. Thanks to those who have encouraged me in writing these daily devotionals. Thanks to those who have supported this work of love by purchasing Volumes I, II, III, and IV.

And thanks to my wife, Kerry. Her love and support have made these books possible. Without her they would have never been written. Blessings to you all!

ABOUT THE AUTHOR

Ron Bowell grew up on the Kansas plains and started playing with rock bands in 1964, traveling for seventeen years with groups like Friar Tuck and the Monks and Coyote. In 2008, Friar Tuck and the Monks were inducted into the Kansas Music Hall of Fame. With the club scene came addiction, but at Christmas time in 1980, Jesus got a hold of Ron's life. This began a season of rapid and profound change. In 1984 he became pastor of the Zion Church near Abilene, Kansas and ministered there fourteen years. In August of 1998 he and his wife, Kerry, moved to Salina, Kansas to plant CrossRoads Church, which quickly became known as the "Rock & Roll Rehab Church". Ron is the producer of the CrossRoads Show, a half hour radio show heard on classic rock stations on Sunday mornings in Salina. He also maintains an internet blog known as "Friar Tuck's Word of the Day" with readers in over eighty nations. Ron and Kerry have five children and fifteen grandchildren. God is good!

Living Beyond Your Means

January 1

Read Acts 1:1-2

The first two verses of the book of Acts give us some important details about Jesus Christ. He lived and died, and then was raised to life again. After His resurrection, He taught His chosen apostles in the power of the Holy Spirit, preparing them for His departure. He was then taken up to heaven by God. In two verses, Luke recognizes the sovereignty of God, establishes the resurrection and the ascension as historical events, and declares the apostles as divinely chosen to establish Christ's church. Many books in the Bible teach what Christianity should look like when lived out in the individual believer. The book of Acts teaches what Christianity should look like when lived out corporately as the church. It is the story of ordinary people trusting in God fully, and being enabled to do things that were far beyond their ability. By faith, they lived beyond their means -- and by faith, we can too.

Dr. Luke - A Giant of the Faith

January 2

Read Acts 1:1-2; Luke 1:1-4

Most Bible scholars agree that a physician named Luke was the author of Acts, and that the "former book" he speaks of is what we know as the Gospel of Luke. He wasn't one of the original disciples, but came to faith early in the church's history. Luke was a physician who accompanied some of the early disciples on their journeys. He is also referred to in several of Paul's epistles. The Gospel of Luke and the book of Acts were likely a two-volume set, written to share the story of Jesus and the early church. Luke had been commissioned by a man named Theophilus. Early in the Gospel of Luke, this man is referred to as "most excellent Theophilus", which indicates that he was a high-ranking government official -- one who had become a seeker of truth. Luke gave him a full dose of Jesus, and if we finish his book, that's what we will also get from this giant of the faith. Thank you Dr. Luke.

Forty Days of Kingdom Preaching

January 3

Read Acts 1:3; John 20:26-31; 1 Cor. 15:1-8

After His resurrection, Jesus spent forty days appearing to people, convincing them that He was alive. He walked among them. He ate and drank with them. They touched Him and listened to Him as He preached about the Kingdom of God. The Kingdom of God is mentioned over fifty times in the Gospels, and was Christ's favorite topic following His resurrection. It is the most important topic we can consider. How we respond to the Lordship of Christ is crucial. It is the most lasting thing about us. How we think of Jesus affects the course of our life, and will determine our eternal destiny. Jesus wants to be more than just our Savior from sin. He also wants to be Lord and King of our life. Only when we live as citizens of Christ's Kingdom can we experience life to its fullest, and live beyond our means spiritually. We never outgrow our need for teaching about the Kingdom of God.

Stay Put

January 4

Read Acts 1:4; Phil. 4:11-13; Jer. 29:11

Even though it was dangerous, the risen Christ told His disciples to stay put and remain in Jerusalem. That may be good advice today, as we struggle with commitment and contentment. Fickle spirits contaminate the church, and we end up changing churches as often as we change our socks. There are various excuses. "I'm not being fed... I don't feel the Spirit... They aren't friendly enough... Somebody ticked me off." But usually, the real reasons go deeper. Maybe we were confronted with a hard truth, or called to change a behavior. Perhaps we were asked to contribute, or maybe we just didn't get our way -- and so we bail. But before we change churches, we should consider changing our hearts. Moving around is not necessarily moving up. If we leave Jerusalem before it's time, we may miss what God has for us. There may be exceptions, but consider staying put for now.

Waiting On God

January 5

Read Acts 1:4-5; Psalm 27:14; Psalm 37:7; Psalm 46:10; Isaiah 40:31

The risen Christ commanded His disciples to stay put and wait for the gift His Father was sending. God's Holy Spirit would soon baptize them, and the power of God would fill their lives. With obedience comes blessing. The Lord still calls us to wait for Him and His blessing. Christ wants to do a work in us as individuals, so that together as the church, we can do His work in this world. God has gifts He wants to give us, truth He wants to teach us, and fruit He wants to grow in us, but we must wait for His timing. It is difficult, but impatience will just bring frustration and defeat. Be still and wait for the Lord. He is God -- wait for what He wants you to have. Your strength will be renewed as you wait upon the Lord, so wait for the gift God is sending. Pray for it, expect it, watch for it, and when it comes, use it for his glory. But today... wait for it.

Stay Focused

January 6

Read Acts 1:6-7; Matthew 24:36-39

As the disciples gathered around the risen Christ, they wanted details about the future. They wanted to know when He would return and restore the Kingdom of God. Jesus told them it was none of their business. His return date was not to take up too much of their time and energy. They were to mind their business, which was establishing the Kingdom of God on earth. That's still good advice. Stay focused on the right stuff. Stop worrying about what is coming next, or when it is coming. Focus on what you can do now. Light up the world with the love of Jesus. Witness to the power of the life changing Gospel with your changed life. Pray for lost people and for one another. Minister to the poor, the weak, the sick, the addicted, and the dying. Help people find Jesus so their lives can be changed, and their souls can be saved. That's our business. That's our mission. Stay focused!

We're on a Mission from God

January 7

Read Acts 1:8; Isaiah 43:10-12

One of John Belushi's famous lines in "The Blues Brothers" movie was, "We're on a mission from God." This is also what Jesus told His disciples. In his final instructions, He told them that God's coming baptism would infuse them with a power they had never had before. They would receive this power so that they could be witnesses for the Kingdom of God in their hometowns, in the cities and states near them, and to nations all over the earth. We too, have been set apart to be His witnesses. We're on a mission from God. When we believe and receive the Holy Spirit, the power of God comes into our lives for a reason: so we can be his witnesses and attract others to His Kingdom. We are called to be His witnesses to those down the road and across the street, and we are to be His witnesses to those in other lands and across the sea. We are on a mission from God!

The Ascension - Taken Up

January 8

Read Acts 1:9; Acts 1:1-2; Luke 24:50-52; Mark 16:19-20

Jesus walked the Earth for some forty days after His resurrection from the dead, teaching His disciples, and giving them some important final instructions. Then, He was taken up to heaven before their eyes. The ascension of Christ is one of the most fantastic stories in Scripture. Jesus gave the disciples one last proof of His divinity. People often ask, "Where is heaven?" We don't know for sure, but we can say with authority that Jesus was "taken up". He didn't go down, nor did He go "poof", and disappear like a magician. He was "taken up to heaven". So whatever and wherever heaven is, we know that Jesus went up to get there. This is the context of the word "ascend". Jesus came down to Earth, and He went back up to be with His Father in heaven. We too will one day ascend to meet the Lord in the air. What a glorious day that will be!

He's Coming Back - Get Busy

January 9

Read Acts 1:10-11; Matt. 24:29-30, 44-46; 1 Peter 2:11-12

As Jesus ascended into the clouds, the disciples stood around, looking up to the sky. Two angels came and reminded them that He would be coming back and expecting results. They had better get busy with the kingdom building stuff Jesus had spoken about. Hadn't He told them it would be good for the servants whose master found them working for Him when he returned? They should stop standing around longing for heaven, and get busy being His disciples here on earth. They were to live every day as if He was coming back today. That's still a good idea! When we do that, the timeline no longer matters. Get out of the holy huddle. Go out and be His witnesses. Stop critiquing and start loving. Do more praising than complaining. Live like Jesus, in the power of the Holy Spirit, and you too can glorify God and live beyond your means.

Obedience

January 10

Read Acts 1:12; Acts 1:4

The term "Christian" has taken a beating in recent years. Some new teachers prefer the term "Christ Follower". But does it really matter what we call those who believe and follow Jesus? The proof of faith is borne out in the content of our living. The early disciples set the tone. They spent enough time with Jesus to receive His teaching, and then, at great risk to their lives, they actually did what Jesus said to do. He told them to "stay in Jerusalem", and that's what they did. After His ascension, they returned to Jerusalem. Were they "Christians" or "Christ Followers"? Call them what you will, the hallmark of their faith was obedience to Christ. Will you spend enough time in prayer and in God's word this year to really hear Him? Will you obey what you hear? As long as God can call us "obedient", it won't really matter what the movers and shakers decide to call us.

Disciples Don't Quit

January 11

Read Acts 1:13; Matt. 10:1-4; John 17:5-12

It is amazing that eleven of Christ's twelve original disciples remained together after His death. They had been scattered at His arrest, and it would have been easy to remain that way. They could have gone back to what they were doing before they met Jesus. Their leader had been killed, their lives were in danger, and there was enough collective guilt in their group to sink a ship. But three years of being with Jesus, and witnessing His resurrection, had changed them. They didn't quit because they had become true followers of Christ. This is a great testimony for us today. Disciples don't quit! The church today has its fair share of "flash in the pan" Christians -- "fair weather" wannabes who hang around with Jesus as long as it's convenient, easy, and fun. They were around in Christ's day too, but deserted Him when the teaching got hard. Don't be found among them. Don't quit!

Christ's Family Gets It

January 12

Read Acts 1:14; Mark 3:20-21; John 7:1-5

There are many miracles found in Acts, including Christ's brothers coming to faith. Mary had pondered her Son's greatness, but His brothers had been antagonistic. Early in Christ's ministry they even tracked Him down in order to take Him home with them. They believed He had lost His mind. The delusional and grandiose things He said about Himself seemed ludicrous to them. But as time went by, and they heard of the miracles and the healings, their hearts must have softened a bit. Scripture tells us that the risen Jesus appeared to His mother, Mary, and to His brother, James. It was likely through their testimony that the rest of Christ's family came to faith. There is a lesson here for us. Do not give up on family members who refuse to believe the Gospel. Continue to be love and light. If the risen Christ lives in us, our family may yet see His glory -- even if it happens after our death.

It is Written

January 13

Read Acts 1:15-20; Psalm 69:25; Psalm 109:8

Peter emerged as an early church leader. He stood up, and he spoke up. He addressed the growing number of Christ followers with a message regarding Judas the betrayer. As a leader with integrity, he didn't sweep failure under the rug. As a godly leader, he set an early precedent -- when he spoke, he spoke from the authority of Scripture. Peter found verses in the Psalms that applied to the betrayer, along with a word about what to do next. The Bible is not just for moral teaching. It can help us make sense of events that happen in our lives, and give us direction about what to do in times of loss, trouble, stress, and betrayal. But we cannot know "it is written", unless we read the word and become intimately acquainted with it. Read the Bible daily in large and small doses. Ditch the excuses and distractions and make knowing God's word a priority in your life. It is written!

Witnessing to the Resurrection

January 14

Read Acts 1:21-22; Romans 1:1-4

Peter listed two criteria for the man who would replace Judas. First, he would need to have been with them since the beginning of Christ's ministry. More than just the twelve faithfully followed Jesus. Second, he would need to have personally witnessed the resurrection, for the resurrection was the foundation stone of the early church. It's where they took their stand. It defined who believed. It validated Jesus as Lord and Savior. It changed the disciples into people who would die for Jesus. They witnessed to it at the cost of their very lives. It was their story, and they stuck to it. Is it your story? Would you give your life to share a testimony of Christ's resurrection in you? Is it still the foundation stone of your church? What has the risen Jesus done in you? Witness to it! The world knows plenty about what the church is against. Now let's tell them who we live for, and why.

Sovereign God

January 15

Read Acts 1:23-26, 1:15-16, 4:24-28

The early church believed in the sovereignty of God so strongly that they literally "drew straws" to choose the disciple who would replace Judas. Rather than voting, which would have reflected their choice, they "cast lots", trusting God to choose, because they believed that God is sovereign. They did their part by offering two godly men, but left the final decision up to their Sovereign Lord. Earlier in Acts, Peter declared that the betrayal of Judas was a fulfillment of Scripture. God's word said it would happen, and it happened -- because God is sovereign. Later in Acts, the apostles spoke of Herod and Pilate conspiring against Jesus. They declared it the fulfillment of God's will -- God is sovereign. Is this the God you believe in? Is He the Sovereign Lord of your life? Do you give God opportunities to lead you, or do you run ahead of Him? Are you walking in His sovereign will, or in yours?

Prayer That Works

January 16

Read Acts 1:24 & 1:14; Rom. 12:12; Phil. 4:6

The early church prayed constantly because they believed that God is sovereign. They trusted God enough to pray that His sovereign will would be revealed to them, and that it would be worked out in their lives. They wanted to be in the will of God more than they wanted anything else. One of the reasons so many Christians are confused about the will of God these days is that they seldom get down to seeking God's will in prayer. Couple that with a general apathy about spending time in God's word, and you end up with sheep who can be led around by almost any shepherd who tickles their ears. They operate by feelings, instead of by the word and prayer. Sincere prayer, coupled with time in the word, can lead us to where God wants us to be. Get back to prayer -- not to get what you want, but to discern what God wants you to have.

All Together In One Place

January 17

Read Acts 2:1; Romans 15:5-6; Psalm 133:1

On that first Pentecost after Christ's ascension, the disciples were "altogether in one place". They stuck together and waited on God. When the Spirit came to fill and embolden the church, they were "altogether in one place". Not only does the Holy Spirit bring unity, unity brings the Holy Spirit. It is difficult for God to dwell in a church filled with dissension. God's Spirit works best where there is harmony. This is why power struggles and infighting are so destructive in the church. It's why God tells us to continuously work at reconciliation between one another. We can't be "all together in one place" when we're busy backstabbing one another. But when the church lives and works together in unity, good things happen as His Spirit moves in power. Petty divisions and personal agendas fade in their importance, and Christ is glorified. What true disciple would not want to see that happen?

Communicating God's Wonders

January 18

Read Acts 2:2-8

When the Holy Spirit came at Pentecost, God sounded like wind and looked like fire -- there was no "small, still voice" that day. The city was filled with pilgrims from every nation, and the Spirit enabled the apostles to speak of His wonders in their languages. The power of God also enabled people from every nation to hear of His wonders in their language. Those who spoke were important, but the big story in these verses is those who heard. God's gift to the apostles was significant, but it had a purpose: to share His wondrous gospel with people who had not yet heard. The gift was not a "perk" -- it was a tool, a means to an end. The Message takes priority over the messengers and the gift that was given to them. How is your "Jesus language"? Can people understand you? Are you communicating God's truth in a language people can comprehend? Ask for God's help.

Mocking God

January 19

Read Acts 2:13; Matthew 27:37-44

When God's Spirit came in power, many people still did not get it. All they heard was gibberish. They mocked the disciples, saying, "Don't listen to them, they're just a bunch of drunks." They were probably some of the same people who mocked Jesus as He died for their sins on the cross. We can learn from this. We won't be able to speak everyone's language, even with God's help. Some will just never hear. Don't expect everyone to react with enthusiasm when you share your witness. Many will write you off as an idiot, or as one under some kind of spell. They will ridicule your faith. They mocked Jesus and the disciples -- they will mock you. When the Spirit comes in power to change your life and your language, many will still mock the work of God. They will cover their ears and shake their heads. But keep speaking God's language, because some will hear. Some will hear!

Called to Preach

January 20

***Read Acts 2:14-20; Acts 9:17-20;
1 Corinthians 9:16; Isaiah 61:1-3***

When the Holy Spirit comes in power, someone will be called to preach. Here, it was Peter -- later it was Paul -- eventually, it may be you. Peter had no formal training, but God compelled him to preach. Preaching can take many forms, from exposition of the Scriptures, to one-on-one witnessing about what God has done in our lives. Peter opened the Scriptures in a new way, and told the mockers that they were not hearing drunken speech, but the voice of God. He proclaimed the sovereignty of God and the amazing grace of the Lord. He told them that their prophets had seen this day coming, and that the Holy Spirit was being poured out for all people. No one would be excluded from the chance to accept God's grace. That's still true today. Jesus calls us to receive Him, and then calls us to preach the gospel in some way.

Everyone Who Calls

January 21

Read Acts 2:21; John 3:16;
Psalm 116:1-6; Genesis 12:7-8

Acts 2:21 is one of the most generous verses in Scripture. "Everyone" can be saved, if we call on the name of the Lord. It's an echo of John 3:16, where Jesus says, "Whoever believes in Him will have eternal life." Salvation and eternity are available to all who believe God and call upon the name of the Lord. What does it mean to call upon the name of the Lord? It means that in desperation, we cry out, "Save me Lord." But it's more than just asking to be saved. It entails a pursuit of God's blessing. In our heart, we build an altar for the Lord, and lay our life on it. We acknowledge the Lordship of Christ, and submit ourselves to His authority and to His sovereign will. "Calling on the name of the Lord" involves more than just a little prayer. It means a total surrender to Jesus. This is the way of faith and salvation. This is the way to eternal life.

Preaching the Gospel

January 22

Read Acts 2:22-23; 1 Corinthians 1:20-25

After Peter had straightened out the mockers on the power of the Holy Spirit, he began to preach the gospel. The gospel according to Peter consisted of two parts: the bad news and the good news -- our need, and God's grace filled solution. Peter defied all modern calls for a positive introduction to his sermon and began with the bad news -- Jesus had died because of them. He later shared the good news that Jesus had also died *for* them, but he started by looking them in the eye and telling them that Jesus had died because of them. We could have easily been standing with them on that day, because that's still a true statement. Jesus died because of us. Our sins nailed Jesus to that cross. We will seldom grasp the depth of God's love and mercy, until we understand that Jesus died because of us. This truth should rid us of all spiritual smugness.

He is Risen

January 23

Read Acts 2:24-32; 1 Cor. 15:12-22

The foundation of our faith is the resurrection of Jesus Christ. The early church rose up declaring this truth. They didn't just believe it -- they lived and died for it because they were witnesses of the fact. In the church's first sermon, Peter declared its centrality. He preached that death could not keep Jesus down. By God's power, Christ had risen from the dead. Peter noted that the great Jewish hero, King David, had seen the resurrection coming and had spoken of it. Don't miss the fact that Peter explained current events of his day by looking deeply into God's word. But more than David's prophecy, Peter declared that he and many others were witnesses to Christ's resurrection. It wasn't just theory -- it happened, and they had seen it. This was a bold and dangerous statement that put the lives of the apostles on the line. They were willing to testify to what God had done. Are you?

Lord and Christ

January 24

Read Acts 2:33-36; Matthew 26:62-68; Romans 10:8-11

Peter preached that God had made Jesus both Lord and Christ. This is the declaration that got Jesus killed, and the truth the apostles would be martyred for teaching. These words can still get you killed. People are beheaded, stoned, or thrown off tall buildings for believing this. At the minimum, you will likely be ostracized and ridiculed for witnessing to this truth. Why? Because, if Jesus really is both Lord and Christ, we must do what He says. He is the Boss. You cannot ignore His words just because they are inconvenient or difficult. You cannot selectively obey someone who is both Lord and Christ. We serve Him. We bow down to Him. If you preach this truth, and live it out today, you will likely be persecuted. But it's still the truth, and Peter was willing to risk his life and his reputation to preach it. We should be willing to do the same.

Cut to the Heart

January 25

Read Acts 2:37; John 16:6-8

Peter boldly preached the truth. What happened next was truly divine. God's Holy Spirit convicted those who heard Peter's message. They were cut to the heart and began to cry out for mercy. They experienced a conviction that only the Holy Spirit can produce. Preachers and witnesses take note: there is a fine line between laying guilt on someone and leading them toward godly conviction. Earthly guilt can only take people so far -- heavenly conviction can take them all the way to Jesus. Carnal guilt drives people away -- godly conviction brings them to the foot of the cross. Guilt is used to manipulate, and keeps people in bondage -- godly conviction is designed to set us free. Anyone can dish out guilt -- a few are gifted to help God do surgery on hardened hearts, which promotes true healing. When the Holy Spirit is involved, it's a good thing to be cut to the heart.

Calling for a Response

January 26

Read Acts 2:38; Acts 26:20; Matt. 3:1-6

The gospel always calls for a response. When Peter preached the gospel, people asked what they could do. He said, "Repent and be baptized." Those who came to hear John the Baptist were called to repent and be baptized. Paul's preaching called for repentance and a response in keeping with repentance. Jesus called people to repent and to follow Him. Repentance demands a change of heart and a change of direction. Baptism is the genuine response of a repentant heart. It's not something that saves people -- it's something that saved people do. It's an act of obedience for those who declare Jesus both Lord and Christ, and who ask Him to wash away their sin. Peter promised that if the people responded to God, God would respond to them and send them the Holy Spirit. The gospel always calls for a response -- and if you respond to God, He will respond to you.

For the Far Off and the Far Out

January 27

Read Acts 2:39; Acts 2:21; Mark 16:14-16

The Lord is calling. He was calling those in Jerusalem on the day of Pentecost, and He went to great lengths so they could hear Him. God is still calling us -- and still going to great lengths so that we can hear Him. The gospel of Jesus Christ is meant for all creation to hear. The Holy Spirit doesn't wait for us to find Jesus. He sends out His word to us while we are still far off. Some of us were even "far out" when we heard the Lord calling. But the call came in, and the Spirit gave us ears to hear. God will call anyone he chooses to call -- high or low, far off or far out. If you have heard His call, or you are hearing it today, that means you have been chosen by God. His call is for you and your children, and it is not wise to ignore it. His promises will never be broken, nor will they be forgotten. So whether you are far off or far out, answer His call. We only get so many chances to do so in a lifetime.

Church Growth

January 28

Read Acts 2:40-41; Matt. 8:11-12; Dan. 12:10

We have a portion of Peter's Pentecost sermon here in Acts. He spoke "many other words". In what we have, you don't hear any "seeker sensitive" stuff. He preached the truth in love, calling people to repent, and to be saved out of their corrupt generation. Then comes this phenomenal evangelism report -- 3,000 were saved. If Peter preached one sermon, and 3,000 were saved, surely we can lead a few people to Jesus in our lifetime. Christians, God has left us here for a reason. Jesus said, "You will be my witnesses." Are you living in a way that anyone would notice Christ in you? Does your life invite people to Jesus, or are you more of a repellant? If you are among those who have not responded publicly to Jesus, let Him save you from this corrupt generation. Be added to the number who will stand before God with His mark and His name. Repent! Today is the day of salvation.

Devotion

January 29

Read Acts 2:42; Matt. 6:24; Ezek. 33:31-32

Acts 2:42 says, "They devoted themselves." The Greek word translated "devoted" means "to latch onto and refuse to let go." The early Christians "latched onto" Jesus and this new group called "the church", and they refused to let go. The Lord wants us to be fully devoted to Him and His Bride, the church. He wants us to love Him with all our heart, mind, soul, and strength. He wants us to latch onto him and not let go. He wants us to love our brothers and sisters in the church in the same way. This is devotion, and even though it is not in vogue today, it is God's desire for every believing heart. In a world where long term commitment is rare, and loyalty has little stamina, Jesus calls us to exceptional devotion. Are you "latched onto" Jesus and His Church with a "never let go" commitment? It's a daily choice that can lead to a lifetime of devotion. Devote yourself today, and refuse to let go.

The Apostles' Teaching

January 30

Read Acts 2:42; Acts 4:33; Eph. 2:19-20

Anyone can be devoted -- it's who or what you are devoted to that is important. The apostles were devoted to Christ and the gospel. They testified constantly to His resurrection. They shared of His love and grace. They conveyed the teaching of Jesus. They preached the word of God. Those who believed became devoted to the teaching of the apostles, which centered on Christ. Are you devoted to the teachings of Jesus found in the word of God? How much time do you spend in the word? Do you really study it and meditate on it? Do you live it out? How much influence does it have in your life? If Jesus looked at your interaction with Him and His word, would He say that you were devoted to the apostles' teaching, which in reality is His teaching? Stop dissecting the word of God and become devoted to it. There's a big difference between the two.

The Fellowship

January 31

Read Acts 2:42; 1 John 1:3, 6-7; 2 Cor. 13:14

Scripture says the early church was devoted to "the fellowship". This term was used for those who made up the local church. Instead of being self-centered, they became community centered. It is amazing what we can get past when we have someone else's benefit at heart. Soldiers often have strong differences with fellow soldiers, but they remember who the real enemy is, and they stick together. They have each other's back. Differences are minimized when there is a common mission. The early church was much the same. Getting our way is less important when our wills are bent toward the good of the community. Unfortunately, rather than watching our back, the church is often known as a place where someone stabs us in the back. This should not be. It is not God's will for the church. The early church was devoted to the fellowship. That calling has not changed.

Breaking Bread

February 1

Read Acts 2:42, 46; Rom. 12:4-5; Eph. 4:4-6

There is a difference of opinion among Bible scholars as to whether the phrase "breaking of bread" speaks of the celebration of the Lord's Supper, or of the practice of eating together in one another's homes as family would do. Either way, the early church lived in a state of constant communion. Whether they broke bread in the church or in their homes becomes secondary to the fact that they bonded as family around their Lord and Savior Jesus Christ. They were in a holy communion with one another, and being together in community around a common table became central to the life of the early church. In our fragmented age, where individual agendas take priority over the common good, we could use a dose of this communal thinking. Having a common Lord should move us toward a common life. Christ founded the church to be His body: one Lord, one faith, one body.

Early Prayer

February 2

Read Acts 2:42; Acts 1:14; Luke 18:1; Philippians 4:6; 2 Chronicles 7:14

The early church was not just about worship, teaching, miracles, and community -- it was also about prayer. They were devoted to prayer, and prayed constantly. They believed that prayer could change things. They saw it work in the lives of people. They prayed for the dead to be raised, and life returned to corpses. They prayed that their witness would draw others to Christ, and people came to the Lord in droves. They would even be seen praying as their bodies perished in the flames and as they were torn apart by wild beasts. They prayed together, and it changed the world. Prayer still changes things, and is vital to the church. We would be wise not to forsake it. The church has enemies who work against it on a daily basis. Will you be one who prays for the church daily? Will you take the time this week to join with other believers in prayer?

Wonders and Awe

February 3

Read Acts 2:43; Luke 7:16; Hebrews 12:28-29; Habakkuk 3:2

When we become devoted to God's word, to the church, and to prayer, miracles happen. There may be healings, signs, and wonders, but often the miracle is a changed life. Drunks sober up. Fools become wise. Haters are moved to love. When God moves in a visible way, people will be in awe. Jesus saved you so that someone could be awed by His grace. It starts with us, as we stand in awe of God's love and mercy in our lives. It spreads to those around us as people begin to see the changes in us, and they are affected by the visible work of Jesus. The response won't always be positive -- the Gospel is a threat to some. But when God's people live out their faith in positive ways -- when we put the word of God into practice, love our neighbors, pray with power, and live in Christian community, many will be filled with awe.

Sticking Together

February 4

Read Acts 2:44-45; John 13:34-35; 1 Cor. 1:10

Jesus brought people together. Those who truly followed Him became like family. They didn't just get a spiritual buzz on Sunday morning, and then go their separate ways -- they stuck together, and cared for one another. They lived for one another and died for one another. They were generous with one another. Detaching themselves from property and belongings, they sold their personal possessions, and helped those among them who were in need. They considered the needs of others as equal to their own. This was more than a church with a lighted sign, a great band, and a radio show -- this was genuine community. We desperately need this today. In a world of small commitments, broken promises, and a myriad of choices, sticking together is harder than ever before. But there is divine power in it. It's the Jesus way, and it is the way of the genuine disciple. Stick together!

Rethinking Church

February 5

***Read Acts 2:46; 2 Corinthians 6:14;
Ephesians 2:19-22; Hebrews 10:25***

Togetherness is the natural result of being "one
in Christ". You can't really "do" togetherness in
an hour on Sunday morning -- it takes more time
than that. The early Christians met together
every day in the temple courts, and they "broke
bread" together in smaller groups in their homes.
They prayed together, studied together, worked
together, ate together, played together, laughed
together, and cried together. They were not only
brothers and sisters, they became friends. They
unyoked from those who did not believe, and
became yoked together with Christ and with one
another. For us to do this, we will need to rethink
what we mean by "church". We'll need to see it
less as a building or a meeting, and begin to see
it as an existence and an identity. "Church" must
become more than just a place or a doctrine. It
must become "who we are".

Positive Christianity

February 6

Read Acts 2:46-47; Rom. 15:13; Eph. 5:1-2

The new believers were positive people. They were "Praise the Lord!" kind of Christians. They had good things to say about each other and about their neighbors. They were short on gossip and long on encouragement. They built one another up instead of tearing one another down. They loved each other with the love they had received from the Lord. And it was noticed. Scripture says they enjoyed the favor of those around them, and the church grew. Positive people draw crowds. Positive people inspire us. We like to be around positive people. It's easy to be a negative critic. It takes spiritual maturity to be a positive witness in the face of a negative world. But God can help. Maybe it's time to change your attitude and become the kind of Christian who draws people to the Lord, instead of fulfilling all the negative stereotypes the world has about the church. It's a matter of the will.

A Growing Church

February 7

Read Acts 2:47b; Matthew 13:18-23

The church grows when people answer God's call to repent and surrender their lives to the Lordship of Christ. When people stop running from God and turn to Him in repentance, the church grows. In the early church, people didn't get saved weekly -- they got saved daily. That is what happens in a church devoted to God's word, to community, and to prayer. That is what happens in a body of believers who concentrate on praise and expressions of devotion and worship. That is what happens when the people of God have a positive attitude about their church and live out their faith in love on a daily basis. That is what happens when the Spirit of God pervades the atmosphere of a church. This is still the kind of church Jesus calls us to be. This is the church that multiplies as the Lord adds daily to their number, producing a crop "a hundred, sixty, or thirty times what was sown."

A Praying Church

February 8

Read Acts 3:1; 1 Thess. 5:16-18; Heb. 13:15-16

Peter and John were going to a prayer meeting at three o'clock in the afternoon. The desire of the early church was to be God-dependent, not self-sufficient. They prayed continually. Today's culture worships at the altar of self-sufficiency. This hinders our desire to pray continually. We can obtain much of what we need without asking God for it -- no need for "daily bread" prayers. The majority of our prayers express a desire for personal blessing, rather than the desire to bring glory to God. Trusting God <u>for</u> all things, and <u>in</u> all things, is what set the early Christians apart. When they prayed, they prayed big and wide. They prayed for God to be glorified in their lives, even if it meant persecution. They just wanted more of God. When we begin to pray for God to be glorified in our lives, God will involve us in the miraculous, and give us opportunities to amaze the world, just like He did with the early church.

Crippled from Birth

February 9

Read Acts 3:2; Psa. 51:5; Job 15:14; Isa. 53:6

Imagine being totally dependent upon others for survival. This needy man, "crippled from birth", had to be carried to the Temple gate so that he could beg for survival. In a way, this helpless beggar represents us all, for we have all been "crippled from birth" by sin. Sin takes our legs out from under us, and we join those begging at the gate of God, unable to enter on our own. We end up looking to people, instead of God, for our sustenance. We spend our lives in spiritual squalor, sitting in our sin, pleading for the crumbs that the world occasionally gives us. We desperately need the Lord, but continually beg others to give us what we think we need. We plead for handouts instead of healing. We become focused on survival instead of seeking salvation. But we can be changed. We can be born again if we trust the Great Physician. Why beg another day? Take God's hand and rise up.

Asking for the Right Stuff

February 10

Read Acts 3:3; James 4:1-4

When Peter and John approached the Temple gate, a beggar, crippled since birth, asked them for money. He was asking for the wrong thing. He asked for money, but what he really needed was healing. It's hard to blame him -- it's an old attitude. Most of us have been conditioned to believe that more money will fix our problems and make us happy -- so even today, many of us are still asking God for the wrong stuff. We ask Him for money, when what we really need is healing -- physical, emotional, and spiritual healing. We plead for pennies, when God has millions to give. We sit begging at the gate of glory, when we could be walking free with Jesus. We wallow in self pity, when the confidence of Christ is ours for the asking. We spend our days asking God just to get by, when what He wants to do is miraculously amaze the world through us. Are you asking God for the right stuff?

Looking the Right Direction

February 11

Read Acts 3:4-5; Matt. 6:22-23; Psa. 121:1-2

At an early age, infants learn to look into our eyes for information and intimacy. Something spiritual happens when we look people in the eye. So it was with the beggar at the gate. Conditioned by years of shame, he kept his head down and didn't look up. It was safer for his soul not to make eye contact. His posture portrayed weakness, defeat, and humiliation. But Peter demanded eye contact, because he knew that God wanted to heal more than just this man's body. Peter and John could have given him a small coin and felt good for helping the poor like many Christians do today. But they wanted to give him more than that. They wanted to give him his life back. They wanted God to heal his soul. So the man looked up and his life was never the same… because when he looked into their eyes, he was looking into the eyes of Christ. The first step to healing is looking up.

Giving What We Have

February 12

Read Acts 3:6; Luke 21:1-4

Peter and John had little in the way of earthly riches, but they were willing to give what they had -- and what they had was Jesus. Jesus is better than silver and gold. Silver and gold only last for a while -- Jesus is forever. Money will only buy stuff that breaks and wears out -- Jesus is eternal. The beggar asked for something that would get him by for today -- Peter and John gave him something that would last for eternity. He wanted something to help him survive -- they showed him how to really live. He wanted them to support his way of life -- they gave him a new life. He was looking for a handout -- Peter and John gave him a hand up. Jesus still calls us to give what we have. Do you have Jesus? If you have Jesus, are you giving Him away, or are you hoarding Him? Give what you have. God will take care of the rest.

Partners with God

February 13

Read Acts 3:7; Acts 9:17-19; Psalm 18:16

Peter reached down and took the crippled beggars hand. This is a potent reminder of how God wants to work through us. God could have just spoken a word and the beggar would have been healed. But God had Peter reach down and take his hand. God has chosen us to be His partners. We are His helping hands. We do the reaching and the preaching. Jesus does the healing. Silver and gold could never have purchased new legs for this man, but Jesus filled his life with healing and dancing because Peter reached down and took his hand. God can do great things through those who will partner with Him by doing small things. Don't just pray for the hungry -- go work in a soup kitchen. Don't just pray for the lost -- reach out to them in love and share the gospel with them. We are partners with Jesus. If we expect Him to do it all, we are in a dysfunctional relationship.

Praise and Amazement

February 14

Read Acts 3:8-10; Matt. 9:33; Matt. 15:31

When we obey God, glory comes down and praise goes up. This ex-cripple was not subtle or sophisticated in his witness. He was ecstatic and out of control. He jumped up and down and danced around, shouting out praises to the Lord. Healed people praise God. Saved people tell of his wonders and mercy. God didn't heal this man because He felt sorry for him and wanted him to have a better life. He didn't heal him so Peter and John could rake in money for their ministry. God healed this man to bring glory to His name. God healed him so people would be amazed at the power to be found in the name of the risen Jesus. Dead men can't heal anyone -- but a risen Lord can. God has come to earth and lives in the changed lives of His people today. He wants us to share our story -- maybe even dance and sing and shout about it. He wants us to give Him glory. How are you doing at that?

Who Gets the Credit?

February 15

Read Acts 3:11-16l; John 20:30-31

After Peter and John brought healing to the cripbled man, the crowd began to treat them as superheroes with great power. It was a test for them. They had to decide whether to accept the glory for themselves, or give glory to God. They passed the test. They declared that faith in the name of Jesus caused the miraculous healing. Human beings are interesting. We excel at holding grudges. We blame God for the tragedies, disasters, and calamities in our lives. Some are still angry at God for something that happened decades ago. But when blessing comes our way, or something good happens in our life, we are prone to explaining it away as coincidence, or worse yet, to taking credit for it ourselves. We chalk it up to being godly, or smart, or just plain lucky. In this world, God gets most of the blame, but not much of the credit. Be different, Christian. Give God glory in all things.

Running To The Church

February 16

Read Acts 3:11; Mark 3:7-10

In a day when people are leaving the church in droves, it's good to see some running to the church in the third chapter of Acts. The same happened to Jesus. The common denominator is the miraculous transformation of lives, and that those who witnessed the deliverance and healing talked it up. This caused many to be astonished and come running to the church. They didn't all stay, but they could never say they had not seen and heard the truth. The same thing can happen today. When people hear about miraculous transformations, they tend to come running. The miracle of a changed life, whether that change is spiritual or physical, can bring glory to God and draw people to the church. When the church does amazing things, people will come running to see what's up. But we have to talk it up out in the world where it really counts. We have to get the word out.

Hanging On or Hanging Out

February 17

Read Acts 3:11; Luke 10:38-42, 19:47-48

The healed beggar hung on to Peter and John. He had been walking, and jumping, and praising God, so it wasn't for stability that he hung on to them. Perhaps it was gratitude for the men who had looked him in the eye and reached down to help him up. He wanted everyone to meet these men who had shown him Jesus and given him a second chance. We can learn from him. He was into hanging on, rather than just hanging out. Jesus needs disciples who will hang on to him, not just hang out with him. He needs people who will hang on His words, not just hang out at church. Many people hung out with Jesus, but it was the disciples who hung on to Him. Jesus is looking for Christians who will hang onto him -- believers who won't forget where they received healing and the words of life -- disciples who will introduce Him to their friends and neighbors. Are you hanging on, or just hanging out?

Pointing People Upward

February 18

Read Acts 3:12-13; Acts 14:11-15; 1 Cor. 10:31

Human beings are plagued by the tendency to worship other humans instead of God. "Celebrity worship" is rampant, whether it be for politicians, athletes, actors, musicians, or preachers. Some will always worship the miracle worker instead of the Miracle Maker. Peter nipped this attitude in the bud. He let people know that it was the living Christ who had healed this man. Peter and John understood that who gets the credit is a big deal. It's the difference between being a disciple and becoming an idol. They pointed people to Christ. They wanted God to get the glory. They wanted the name of Jesus to be praised. This was their mission and purpose in life. The same goes for us. We all have opportunities to glorify the Lord. God is still glorifying Jesus Christ through those who choose to give Him glory. Everything believers do should be done to the glory of God. Point people upward!

The Forbidden "You" Message

February 19

Read Acts 3:13-17; Matt. 23:27-28; Isaiah 30:10-11

Peter preached to the crowd gathered around the healed beggar, and he did something that modern preachers are told never to do -- he preached a "you" message. He pointed his prophetic finger at them and said, "You sinned and you need to change your ways." Pastors are told not to preach that way today. People want "positive" messages. But Peter threw caution to the wind, and said: "You handed Jesus over to be killed. You disowned him. You asked for a murderer to be spared instead of Christ. You killed the author of life. You acted ignorantly." WOW! That would empty a church sanctuary today. But what if it's the truth? What if God wants you to know your sins and wants you to change? In a way, every message from the Holy Spirit is personal. You can't receive personal salvation and then refuse to receive personal messages. God is speaking to you. Repent!

There's Power in the Name

February 20

Read Acts 3:15-16; Luke 24:45-48

Christians serve a risen Savior, and because of the resurrection, there is power in the name of Jesus. As witnesses of the resurrection, the early apostles preached of His lordship, His salvation, and His healing. They proclaimed that there was power in the name of Jesus, and that by faith in His name, people could be healed, delivered, and saved. They preached the gospel of salvation. We are called to the same ministry. We must tell people that sin has crippled them and will kill them. We must tell them that God raised Jesus from the dead, and that we are His witnesses because the risen Christ has changed our lives. We must tell them that there is power in the name of Jesus and call them to repent and put their faith in His name. He is the One who can heal our crippled hearts, deliver us from our demons, and forgive our sins. Jesus saves! There is power in the name of Jesus.

The Eternal Gospel

February 21

Read Acts 3:17-26; Hebrews 8:10-12

Peter used the healed beggar to share the eternal gospel -- a gospel that never changes because it comes from an unchanging and eternal God. He called them to repent and turn to God from their wicked ways. They had sinned and fallen short of the glory of God -- something we have all done. Turning to God would wipe out their sins. The Lord would remember their sins no more. We all need this! Not only would their sins be forgiven, but times of refreshing would come from the Lord. In a dry and weary land, they would have living water. The risen Christ would come to live in them, and their lives would be transformed. Turning to Jesus would not only save them, it would also empower them to be obedient to God and His word. Jesus would become Lord of their lives and they would become Christ-followers. This is the eternal gospel. Have you believed it? Are you living it?

A Disturbing Gospel

February 22

Read Acts 4:1-4; Matthew 2:1-3

When one proclaims that God has come to Earth as Lord and Savior for all mankind, the "powers that be" will be disturbed. When one preaches that wicked men killed Christ, but God raised Him from the dead, evil will rise up to silence you -- for if Jesus died for our sins and was raised from the dead, we would be fools not to worship and serve Him. Earthly powers will agree that Jesus was a good person and a great teacher, but they cannot tolerate Him as God incarnate. Those in authority are threatened by those who will bow down only to Christ. Man's autonomy is challenged when we preach that salvation is found in Christ alone. A gospel that gives people only two choices for eternity is a disturbing gospel, and if we preach it, like Peter and John, we will be marginalized, harassed, and even punished. But if we faithfully live it out, some will be saved, and the church will grow.

No Other Name

February 23

Read Acts 4:5-12; John 14:6

Peter and John were called before the rulers to account for the beggar's healing. The elders wanted to know by what power or what name they had done this miracle. Peter was blunt: "The Jesus you killed is alive. He rose from the dead and there is great power in His name. His name not only provided physical healing for this man, there is no other name by which your souls can be saved from hell." Peter is echoing the words that Jesus told His disciples, "I am the way. No one comes to the Father, unless they come through me. I am the only way to Heaven." This is not some narrow-minded bigot speaking -- it is the Lord Jesus Christ. Peter was preaching that Jesus is the Messiah, the Rock of our salvation, the one and only Savior of all mankind. This is still the gospel truth. There is no other way to Heaven. There is no other name that can save us. Believe it! Proclaim it!

Unschooled and Ordinary

February 24

Read Acts 4:13; Acts 2:41-47

The apostles were not highly educated like the Pharisees and the Sanhedrin, but they had an effective ministry. They had no letters following their names, but they had been with Jesus and they had courage. With these godly credentials, they literally changed the world. Education is not the most important factor in effective ministry. Churches that value academic degrees over gifting and calling have forgotten Acts 4:13. Courageous, unschooled, ordinary men, who had been with Jesus, planted churches that grew in number daily. When you couple a close relationship with Christ to a courageous heart, you have a potent combination for effective ministry. Have you been with Jesus? Would anyone look at your life and take note that you have been with Jesus? Are you courageous in sharing your faith? This is how "unschooled, ordinary" Christians change the world.

Effective Ministry = Visible Fruit

February 25

Read Acts 4:14-16; Acts 4:21b; Luke 3:4-6

Effective ministry bears visible fruit that brings glory to God. People are saved. People are baptized. People are healed. People's lives are visibly changed so that everyone can see what has happened. God doesn't do these things so we can feel special or get puffed up -- God does it so we will give Him glory and people will look up. God doesn't change our lives just so we can live better. God changes our lives so we can give Him glory and be His witnesses. When Peter healed the crippled beggar, everybody knew that God had done something really big. The religious leaders couldn't ignore it because everyone was praising God for what they had seen. If our changed lives don't cause people to praise God for what has happened, we have probably been hiding our miracle. Why would we want to do that? Effective ministry bears visible fruit that brings glory to God.

Effective Ministry and Resistance

February 26

Read Acts 4:17-18; Acts 4:21a

Effective ministry will generate some resistance.
When you insist on publicly giving glory to Jesus
Christ, praising and proclaiming His name
outside of the church walls, you will meet with
resistance. The resistance can come in being
shunned. People may avoid you at work. Old
friends stop coming around. You don't receive
all the party invitations you used to receive. Or
the resistance may take on a more hostile
nature. You may be confronted and told in no
uncertain terms to shut up about this Jesus stuff.
You may even be threatened with bodily harm.
This is what happened to Peter and John. But
they remained faithful and continued to speak
the truth in love. Every believer with an effective
ministry will face resistance. Remain faithful!
The resistance we face pales in comparison to
being beaten beyond recognition and nailed to a
cross. Remain faithful and some will be saved.

Effective Ministry and Commitment

February 27

Read Acts 4:19-20; Acts 14:1-7; Luke 19:37-40

At some point, our commitment to Jesus and His message will be tested. If our commitment to sharing the Gospel has never been tested, it is likely we are not faithfully communicating the heart of Jesus. When we are tested, we have a choice to make -- we can fold like a card table or we can stand strong. Peter and John stood strong. They told the authorities, "We cannot help ourselves." They could not stop talking about what they had seen and heard with Jesus. When we come to the point where we "cannot help ourselves", God will give us courage for every situation and we will be empowered to tell people about what we've seen and heard. Effective ministry requires commitment. It will also take the Holy Spirit's power to stand against the public pressure to silence our witness. But if we stand strong, we can have an effective ministry, and souls can be saved. Stand strong!

Effective Ministry is Dependent

February 28

Read Acts 4:23-30; 1 Peter 4:6-7

Effective ministry is powered by a strong dependence upon God and His church. Peter and John gathered the church together, and went before the Lord in prayer. They were team players, not rugged individualists. They praised God for what He had done, and remembered His greatness. They asked for faith and strength to continue doing ministry. We don't hear them asking for protection, or that God would spare them from the penalties of speaking the truth. They asked for the courage to fulfill their calling, regardless of what happened. They asked God to make them effective ministers, and to make them more visible, even though their lives had been threatened. They asked for boldness in preaching. This is the kind of prayer that can change a city, or even the world. And if we desire an effective ministry, this is the kind of prayer disciples should be praying today.

God Answers Prayer

March 1

Read Acts 4:31; Matt. 7:7-8; 1 John 5:14-15

The prayers that shook the building where the disciples had gathered were prayers for courage and boldness to witness in the face of danger. That kind of prayer can still shake the church. When we begin to pray according to God's will as the disciples did, asking the Lord to do great things through us for His glory, He will enable us to speak the word of God boldly, and the church will grow. We may suffer, but God's Kingdom will expand. When we allow God's Spirit to fill us, and when we live with the faith and joy of the early church, we will see awesome answers to prayer. And when God answers prayer, what He has done in our lives will not remain a secret. How the Lord blessed us and changed us will become a part of our normal, daily conversation. The church will grow when genuine faith brings genuine change, and when those genuinely changed share a genuine witness. Speak up!

I Surrender All

March 2

Read Acts 4:32; 2 Corinthians 8:1-5

This Sunday someone, somewhere, will sing the old hymn, "I Surrender All". But almost everyone who sings it has an exception clause or two -- an unwritten list of things we won't surrender. Very likely, that list includes some of our possessions. Soon after Pentecost, the infant church became the most generous institution on the face of the Earth. The early Christians surrendered up their possessions and shared all that they had with one another. Only fully surrendered hearts can bow like this to God's heart. Their hearts had become one -- they now had the heart of Jesus. They not only sold out to Jesus, they sold out for one another. They gave up the right to use the word, "mine". Vanity, envy, and striving for status had no place in their lives. This kind of giving requires divine intervention. Only a heart overflowing with the Holy Spirit can be this generous. May our hearts be filled!

Grace Giving Empowers Preaching

March 3

Read Acts 4:33; 2 Cor. 8:7; 2 Cor. 9:8

Grace giving empowers gospel preaching. The early Christians gave generously to one another as they witnessed to their changed lives, and the apostles continued to testify with great power. This combination of faith and deeds changed the world. The generous church grows -- the stingy church shrivels. Generous Christians grow -- stingy Christians shrivel. Christian witness is muted by a stingy heart, while grace giving opens the doors of heaven. This goes way beyond money -- it's about the joyful and sacrificial giving of one's life, one's time, one's love, one's talent, and one's heart. The church needs Christians who are more concerned with what they can offer the church, than with what the church can offer them -- believers who ask, "What can I give?" rather than, "What can I get?". This is the kind of church the disciples belonged to, and it's a worthy model for today.

New Priorities

March 4

Read Acts 4:34-35; Matt. 19:16-23; Luke 12:32-34

There were no needy persons among those who joined with the early church. They did this by applying a simple principle -- those who had more than they needed, gave to those who did not have enough. Possessions lost their power to captivate as people became disciples of Jesus and were filled with the Holy Spirit. The early believers were more interested in storing up treasure in heaven, than with accumulating wealth here on earth. The needs of the church, supporting those who preached the word, and supplying the needs of the poor, became paramount in the hearts of those touched by the grace of God. Today, spreading the gospel and ministry to our fellow believers should rank above getting our kids the latest iPhone, or having that new car, or those new clothes, or that new sports gear. It's a matter of a new life, with new priorities. It's the Jesus way.

Son of Encouragement

March 5

Read Acts 4:36; 2 Cor. 9:10-13; Rom. 12:1

Today we meet a man named Joseph, who later became known as Barnabas. Eventually, he teamed up with a convert named Paul, and together they took the gospel to much of the Gentile world around the Mediterranean Sea. Barnabas didn't start out to be an apostle. He started out as just an ordinary guy with a generous heart -- a man who had something he was willing to give. He stepped up and gave what he had, while he was still alive, and in the process, modeled what it means to be a "living sacrifice". Today, we think people are generous if they give their stuff away after they die. But after we die, we no longer need our stuff. Generosity is not giving away something that we don't need. Generosity is giving away something we could still use, simply because someone else has a need for it. This is the kind of generosity that will make you a "son of encouragement".

More Than a Tithe

March 6

Read Acts 5:1-2; Acts 4:36; Luke 21:1-4

Spirit filled giving is more than tithing. God blesses the person who tithes, but it is not His intent that we stop there. When God pours out his blessing into our lives he doesn't stop at 10%. You didn't get 10% of God's grace when you came to him for forgiveness -- you got 100% of God's grace. Barnabas gave 100%. The poor widow in Luke's gospel gave 100%. But Ananias withheld part of his offering for himself, and as we will see, the consequences were severe. The amount we give is not important. It's not even really about the percentage. It's our heart that matters. It's the sacrifice that matters. God's intent is that as our walk with the Lord grows stronger, and as we trust Him more and more, we will grow in our willingness to give. As our love for Jesus grows, so will our love of giving. We really will come to believe that we cannot "out give" God, and our actions will prove it.

Holding Back

March 7

Read Acts 5:3; Mark 12:30; Prov. 11:24

God was not pleased with what Ananias offered. God's problem was not with the amount, but with the man. Peter spoke for God, saying: "Satan has filled your heart. You have lied to God and held back money from Him." Ananias appeared generous, but greed had claimed his heart. He didn't trust God to care for his needs, and he held back from God. Many in the church today hold back from God. They hold back on ministry, and others must work harder to get the job done. They hold back on giving, and others must give more to meet the church's needs. They hold back their obedience, and others must go to accomplish the mission. When we stand in front of God, one of His questions might be, "Why did you hold back? I gave you 100%. I gave my all for you. Why did you hold back on me?" How would you answer that question? By the way, there is no good answer.

Living in Awe of God

March 8

Read Acts 5:4-11; Heb. 12:28-29; Hab. 3:2

Ananias and his wife Sapphira lied to God. It is never wise to lie to God. We can deceive people, but we cannot deceive the Lord. What is wise is to live in awe of God's knowledge, power, judgment, and mercy. Do you live in awe of God? Does your giving reflect that awe? Does your service glorify His name? Ananias thought he could lie to God and get away with it. It cost him his life. When we lie to God, we also lose. Our spirits weaken. We become man-pleasers rather than God-pleasers. We withhold more and more from God as time goes by. We may even begin to tell God, "I just don't have it to give right now. I'm giving as much as I can." But God will know better. We cannot thrive spiritually when we lie to God, and Christ's Bride, the Church, suffers when Christians hold back more than they really need for themselves. Live in awe of God.

The Shadows of Our Faith

March 9

Read Acts 5:12-16; Psa. 36:7; Isa. 32:2-4

Many of us grew up hoping we could change the world somehow. We dreamed that our lives would make a difference. God, in his grace, has given us a way to do that. When we dare to walk by faith, people around us will be affected. When the Holy Spirit fills us, our presence in this world will be felt. Just being in Peter's shadow could change someone's life. Think on that for a bit -- living a life so reflective of Jesus that just being in our shadow could bring the healing of God. What kind of shade are you producing? Do others find healing in your shadow? The early Christians had a significant impact on their communities. People were healed, lives were changed, and their numbers grew daily. Is your church producing shade where people can find shelter from the heat and hostility of this world? If not, churches can be changed just like the world is changed -- one life at a time.

High Risk Preaching

March 10

Read Acts 5:17-21; Matthew 10:16-20

The apostles preached and many came to faith in Christ, but not everyone was happy. The Sadducees were jealous, and had the disciples arrested and jailed. But that did not stop these pioneer Christians. An angel freed them and told them to keep preaching. The disciples had a choice: would they leave town and protect their lives, or would they return to preach and face great danger? They chose to obey the angel and continued to witness and teach in Christ's name. This was high risk preaching. Today we worry that people might criticize us or leave the church if we preach the hard stuff. Many a sermon has been "softened" up so as not to offend anyone. Tickling ears is much safer than cutting to the heart. But while we worry about our popularity and jobs, we see the apostles, like sheep among wolves, risking their lives to share the gospel. We would do well to follow their example.

The Full Message

March 11

Read Acts 5:19-20; Rom. 10:17; 2 Tim. 4:17

The angel commanded the apostles to tell people "the full message". The "full message" goes like this. We were created to be with God, but we have all sinned, and our sin separates us from Him. We have all gone astray, but the Lord came looking for us. Jesus came to seek and save the lost. He loved us so much that He paid for all our sins by dying on a cross. To prove that His payment was sufficient, God raised Jesus from the dead. He lives today, and calls us to become His followers. To be saved, we must believe God, and believe that what Jesus did was sufficient. We must put our faith in God's grace and provision. When we believe, we are born again and given a new life. We are called to be Christ's disciples -- to witness to His grace with our changed life. God works through us to call people to Him. This is the "full message" in a nutshell. Have you believed this message?

The Zealous Disciple

March 12

Read Acts 5:21; Romans 12:11; Psalm 69:8-9

The apostles had been jailed for preaching Christ and warned not to teach again in His name. But when the angel freed them, they went right back out and began preaching again. This is zeal for the Lord. Their zeal for obeying God and telling others about Jesus overpowered their natural fear of being chastised, imprisoned, or even killed. Their calling became more important than their personal safety or their personal agenda. When Christ rules in our lives, our zeal for witness grows, and our concern for personal prestige wanes. Our zeal for sharing his name with others multiplies to the point that we can't hold it in any more. Is your zeal increasing or waning? Have you committed your life to being a witness for Christ, or are you more committed to being popular? Was it the "In crowd" who saved you? Or was it Jesus? Allow zeal for Christ to consume you. Become a zealous disciple.

A Dollar Short and a Day Late

March 13

Read Acts 5:21b-25; Isaiah 42:16-25

Religion ruled the lives of those who opposed the apostles -- and when religion rules our lives, we will always be a dollar short and a day late when it comes to the movement of God's Spirit. Focusing on the rules of religion, rather than on their relationship with the Ruler, caused them to be unaware of what God was doing in their time. They didn't get it, and were "puzzled" by God's miraculous delivery of the apostles. Religion blinded them to the workings of God, and deafened them to the gospel. They were more concerned with being in control of the situation, than with being conscious of the Spirit. One of the keys to successful ministry is finding out where God is moving and then going there. We can't do that when we focus on the wrong stuff. When we follow a religion rather than Jesus, we will always be a dollar short and a day late when it comes to sensing the Spirit's moving.

With Power Comes Responsibility

March 14

Read Acts 5:26-28; Matthew 27:15-26

With power comes responsibility. The religious authorities in our Scripture verses today didn't want Christ's name and teaching to spread. They feared they would lose power. If people began following Jesus, they would likely stop obeying the religious big shots in Jerusalem. But while the religious authorities were guarding their power and coveting more of it, they were also denying any responsibility for the death of Jesus -- even though it was their exertion of power that brought about His crucifixion. Christ's blood was on their hands, and on Pilate's. He tried to wash his hands of it, but blood does not come off that easily. An unholy alliance of religion and state had nailed an innocent man to a cross and there was no escaping that truth. Corrupt power always brings death. We would all do well to learn this lesson, because like it or not, with power comes responsibility.

A Dangerous Obedience

March 15

Read Acts 5:29; Acts 4:19-20; Ex. 1:15-21

Acts 5:29 is a dangerous verse. It can make you unpopular, get you arrested, or even get you killed. When we begin to seriously follow Jesus, there will be times when the decrees of our government, or even our church, do not match up with His commands. In those times we have a choice to make -- we can obey man or we can obey God. The Hebrew midwives chose to obey God rather than the king of Egypt. That was dangerous. The apostles declared to the religious authorities that they would obey God rather than man. It was a dangerous obedience. These were the same religious authorities who had killed Jesus. Obeying God rather than man is risky business. It will usually cost us or our family something. We may lose status, friends, money, jobs, or in some instances, even our lives. But in the end, it will be worth the price. Seek God's approval rather than man's.

Passion for the Gospel

March 16

Read Acts 5:30-31; Romans 1:8-17

When Christ rules in our life, zeal to tell our story begins to grow, along with a passion for the gospel message itself. The apostles not only shared their story with the Sanhedrin, they also shared the gospel. With passion they declared, "This Jesus you crucified really came to die for your sins and ours. But God raised him up and offers forgiveness and mercy to those who will repent and acknowledge Him as Lord." In a couple of sentences they shared the gospel along with their personal witness. Could you share the gospel with someone in a couple of sentences? Are you passionate about the gospel? Our lifestyle and personal testimony are only designed to light the way to Jesus. They are like an appetizer. They cannot save people. Without a passion for sharing the gospel, our stories can sound like simple self-glorification. Ask God to give you a passion for the gospel.

Hostility Toward the Name

March 17

Read Acts 5:33; Acts 5:40-42

Throughout the church's history, Christians have been persecuted and killed for witnessing about Jesus. Christ threatened the religious system of His day, and the response of religion is often to eliminate the competition. We see it happening in our world today. On this particular day, in an attempt to silence them, the Sanhedrin had the apostles flogged for preaching the truth. It didn't work. The apostles rejoiced in being found worthy of "suffering disgrace for the Name", and they kept preaching. Will you? The goal of many today is to silence Christians, and eliminate the name of Jesus from the public arena. You can talk profane trash in public, but do not talk about Jesus or you will be flogged. It may be a verbal or emotional flogging, but it may even become physical. If you persist in speaking "the Name", there will be an attempt to disgrace you. Will you wilt, or will you rejoice in being found worthy?

Fighting Against God

March 18

Read Acts 5:34-39; Proverbs 21:30

As Gamaliel spoke to the Sanhedrin, he said something profound. He urged his colleagues not to kill the apostles, because if the gospel they were preaching was from the Lord, the Sanhedrin would end up "fighting against God". The apostles could be flogged, disgraced, hounded, persecuted, and even killed… but if their message was from God, it could not be stopped. Those who fight against God never win in the end. Christians, we need to receive this prophetic statement from Gamaliel as an admonition to us. We have been commissioned to deliver the gospel, God's message of truth, grace, hope, and love. It cannot be stopped. When people try to silence the gospel, they are fighting against God. Do not be intimidated or afraid. We may suffer, but the gospel will be victorious. No one can succeed when they fight against God.

Found Worthy

March 19

Read Acts 5:41; James 1:2-4; 1 Peter 4:12-16

If we were flogged for sharing our faith, most of us would probably file a police report and a lawsuit. The apostles didn't do that. They rejoiced that they had been "counted worthy of suffering disgrace for the Name." They were beaten for preaching the gospel, and praised God for the honor. Being publicly disgraced was acceptable to them, as long as it was disgrace for the Name of Jesus. Many times today, we are disgraced for bad behavior. There is no cause for joy in that. Don't confuse the trouble you go through because of foolish disobedience, for the persecution of the faithful. But we are blessed if we suffer ridicule and disgrace for our witness to the Name of Jesus. So if you have been verbally flogged and ridiculed of late, stop whining and start praising God. You have been found "worthy of suffering disgrace for the Name." You have made the Lord's Honor Roll.

Day After Day

March 20

Read Acts 5:42; Psalm 61:8; Psalm 96:2

The apostles were beaten, threatened with death, and publicly disgraced, but they went right back out the next day and witnessed to the power of the gospel. Day after day, they shared the good news. Day after day, they sang the praises of Jesus. Day after day, they proclaimed His salvation in their church, and from house to house. Day after day, they put the cause of Christ above their personal well being. This is our calling as His disciples. Never stop telling the story that God has come to Earth. The Creator stepped into His creation. His name is Jesus, and He came to redeem our lives and save our souls. Healing and wholeness are found in His name. Forgiveness flows from His grace. His mercy and love are available to all who believe God, and confess that Jesus is Lord. Day after day, the apostles never stopped proclaiming this message. Neither should we!

Church Growth and Factions

March 21

Read Acts 6:1; James 1:27-2:1

The rapid growth of the early church brought with it some problems. The church was called to compassion, and began to provide food for widows who had no other source of income. But in the distribution of that food, some widows were being favored over others, based on their nationality. And so we see, that from the very beginning, the church has struggled with favoritism and factions -- factions which place the emphasis on what group you belong to, rather than on what Lord you belong to. Favoritism is not a product of our times, but of our human nature -- and God calls it a sin. The apostles did not ignore this complaint, but took positive and creative action to see that legitimate needs were met. If the church today is to grow biblically, it must not show favoritism for one group over another. In fact, factions are usually a key factor in the slow death of churches.

Delegating Ministry

March 22

Read Acts 6:2-4; 1 Cor. 12:4-12; Eph. 4:7-11

As the church grew, needs multiplied. To meet those needs, the apostles delegated the hands-on caring ministry to other gifted and mature believers. They would not be sidetracked from preaching the gospel. This may sound like a lack of compassion to us, but their compassion was in their delegation. They recognized a legitimate need, but personally meeting that need was not their primary calling. They had not been called to run a feeding program for the hungry. Their commission was to make disciples of all nations and teach them to obey the Lord. There was no written gospel at that time. The words of Christ were in their hearts and needed to be shared while they were still alive. Their calling was to prayer and to the ministry of God's word. They demonstrated compassion and wisdom by delegating the ministries that were outside of their calling. We would be wise to do the same.

Shared Ministry = Church Growth

March 23

Read Acts 6:5-7; Romans 12:4-8

New workers were chosen to lighten the load on the apostles, and the church grew rapidly. Ministry works best when it is shared. No one can effectively do everything. Spirit filled ministry is a team effort. Growth happens when team members concentrate on their areas of calling and gifting. The church must find ways to help people do what they do best. When leaders wear too many hats, their knees will eventually buckle, and the church will lack vitality. But the church needs more than just workers -- she needs workers who are Spirit-filled Jesus lovers, because Christ is the most important commodity we have to share. We must do more than just fill stomachs to obey the great commission. Compassion that is void of Christ may satisfy our humanity, but it will not glorify God. If we give people food, but fail to give them Jesus, we have failed to be the church.

Full of God's Grace and Power

March 24

Read Acts 6:8-15

Stephen was one of the seven men chosen by the apostles to help oversee the distribution of food for those in need. He also had prophetic gifts and began to preach the word of God with authority. He is described as a man who was "full of faith and full of the Holy Spirit and wisdom" -- "a man full of God's grace and power", who "did great wonders and miraculous signs among the people". The religious experts "could not stand up against his wisdom or the Spirit by whom he spoke". When Stephen spoke, "his face was like the face of an angel". Today we would call Stephen a "superstar". Being a superstar for God will get you noticed, especially by those who oppose the name of Jesus. Stephen faced his persecutors and never flinched. Are you full of God's grace, wisdom, faith, and power? You will face opposition and persecution. Take it as a compliment and shine!

Faith of Our Fathers

March 25

Read Acts 7:1-16

Stephen lifts up the early fathers of faith found in Genesis. Abraham believed God and went where he was told to go. Faith and obedience go hand in hand. His son Isaac became a child of the promise after years of waiting. Isaac's son Jacob, was drawn out of his deceit and into faith, and was given a new name. Jacob's twelve sons eventually grew into that new name, becoming the twelve tribes of Israel. One of them, Joseph, was despised and rejected by his brothers. Sold into slavery, but blessed by God, he rose to become a great leader, and with grace, provided a salvation for the very brothers who had tried to kill him. Believing God; faith and obedience; becoming a child of the promise; getting a new name; finding grace and salvation in one who was thought dead… all these are pictures of faith in Christ. It's a faith we are called to emulate today -- the faith of our fathers.

Full Circle

March 26

Read Acts 7:17-35

Stephen's history lesson continues with Moses. God's people were enslaved in Egypt, but began to outnumber the Egyptians. Pharaoh began a forced infanticide, but baby Moses was placed in a basket, adopted by Pharaoh's daughter, and raised as an Egyptian. At age forty, Moses killed an Egyptian in defense of his people, and fled to Midian. After forty years there, God spoke to him out of a burning bush, commanding him to return to Egypt and become their deliverer and ruler. Moses obeyed. He had come full circle. There are two lessons here. First, when God wants a job done, He prepares His ministers, and waits for the right time to send them. Hurry and haste are not godly traits. Second, when God wants a job done, He often sends someone who has "been there, done that". Don't be hasty in returning to your "Egypt" -- God may send you full circle in His time. Wait on the Lord!

Take Me Back to Egypt

March 27

Read Acts 7:36-43; Deut. 6:10-15; Luke 4:5-8

Moses was sent back to Egypt to free God's people. But after they were set free, they rejected the leadership of Moses. Their bodies had left Egypt, but their hearts had not. Instead of stepping out in faith, they wanted to go back. Being sent back to Egypt by God and desiring Egypt's comforts are two completely different things. As Moses was on the mountain receiving the words of God, the people built a golden calf to worship. Later they chased after false gods like Molech and Rephan, and the Lord gave them over to captivity and exile among the Babylonians and the Assyrians. Stephen's message is clear. When we put our personal Egypt and our idols ahead of God, we surrender our freedom. When our hearts do not fully belong to God, we will eventually enter into exile and captivity. "Worship the Lord your God and serve Him only."

A House for the Creator

March 28

Read Acts 7:44-50; Psalm 139:7-16; 1 Cor. 3:16

How do you build a house for a God who is omnipresent? How can a structure made by human hands possibly hold the Creator of those hands? No temple made by man can contain God. The religionists that Stephen addressed had become proud and arrogant. They thought their theology could contain the God of the universe. They believed their laws were the summation of God's nature, and that their piety made them godlike. They should have known that, even though God instructed Moses in the building of the tabernacle, and Solomon in the construction of the temple, no man made structure can contain a God who is infinite and eternal. The only temple that God lives in is one that He made. God lives in His creation -- in you and me. When we come to faith, Christ comes to live in us. If we believe God, we become God's temple. Take care of that temple.

Truth and Martyrs

March 29

Read Acts 7:51-58; Matthew 23:25-39

Sometimes the truth hurts. Sometimes it can even get you killed. Ask Stephen. Ask the millions of Christians who have been martyred since Christ walked this Earth. After Stephen's brief history lesson, he unloaded on the Sanhedrin. They and their ilk had persecuted and killed many a prophet down through the years. Now they had murdered the Son of God. They had been entrusted with God's Law, but they did not obey it. Stephen held nothing back. Full of God's Spirit, he looked to heaven and declared that Jesus was alive and standing at the right hand of God. He was saying that Jesus is Lord -- Jesus is God. The Sanhedrin went ballistic. They struck back -- not with arguments, but with violence. They stoned Stephen to death and Christianity had its first martyr. Sometimes the truth hurts. It can hurt those who hear it, and it can hurt those who speak it. Speak it anyway.

You Never Know Who's Watching

March 30

Read Acts 7:57-8:1; Luke 23:33-34; Luke 23:46

Stephen looked into the eyes of the most powerful religious leaders in Israel and spoke the truth of God. It wasn't just a slap upside the head -- it was blunt force trauma. He had to have known what would happen. Stiff necked people, with hardened hearts, who resist the Holy Spirit, will kill you. But speaking the truth in love is one of the ways we let our lights shine. You never know who is watching and listening. On this day it was Saul. He saw the angelic face, and heard the voice of forgiveness and mercy. A seed of glory was planted in this future apostle of grace, and he could not uproot it. Stephen let his light shine and Saul couldn't get the light to turn off. Later on that narrow road to Damascus, Saul met the genuine Light of the world. Then he understood Stephen's light. Speak the truth in love. Let your light shine. You never know who's listening and watching.

Scattered For His Glory

March 31

Read Acts 8:1-4; Acts 1:8

Jesus told His disciples that they would be His witnesses to the ends of the Earth. Little did they know that it would be a violent persecution that scattered them like seed in the wind. The infant church had no grand world missions program. It started as simply a matter of survival. As Saul and his cohorts began to intimidate and destroy those of the faith, many were forced to flee for their lives. But Saul's strategy failed. In fact, it actually served to multiply and amplify the message. No one can silence Christianity. One cannot put a bridle and bit on the power of God. Everywhere the new disciples went they shared the gospel and the story of the resurrection. The gospel spread throughout the region because of those scattered disciples. Think about this the next time you end up in a place where you don't want to be, under less than favorable conditions. Perhaps God has you there for a reason.

Amplifying the Gospel

April 1

Read Acts 8:4-5; Joshua 1:9

When the church was scattered under the persecution of Saul, it was as if the volume knob of the gospel had been turned all the way up. Many who could never hear before, could now listen to the greatest story ever told. The scattered believers became a "road show" for Jesus. Wherever they went, the call to be His witnesses remained strong. Their salvation became more important than their survival. Their calling became more important than their comfort. Their Lord became more important than their lives. We should be challenged by their courage and stamina. As the circumstances of life scatter us, let us be among those enduring disciples who share our faith with vigor. As we step out of our church doors each week, may the volume of the gospel increase. And when we stand before God, may it be said of us, "They preached the word wherever they went!"

Philip: the Antidote for Saul

April 2

Read Acts 8:5-7; Romans 12:21

For every Saul, there is a Philip. Saul was into destruction -- Philip was into deliverance. Saul was into mayhem -- Philip was into miracles. Saul was into hurting people -- Philip was into healing people. Saul was into persecuting Christians -- Philip was into preaching Christ. For every tyrant like Saul, there is a saint like Philip. For every Christian intimidated into silence, there are others who will speak up for Jesus. They will confront evil, heal the sick, and take the gospel to the "Samaritans" of this world. You can kill these "Philips", but more will rise up to take their place. The Jesus "genie" is out of the bottle, and the "Sauls" of this world cannot put Him back in. The only question left is, "Will you be a Philip?" Will you take God's power with you, wherever the trials of life send you, and help people receive healing and freedom? For every Saul there is a Philip. Will you be a Philip?

Portable Joy

April 3

Read Acts 8:8; 1 Peter 1:8-9; Gal. 5:22-23

When persecution scattered the early church, the disciples took the joy of the Lord with them wherever they went. As Philip moved through Samaria, joy followed in his wake. One would expect bitterness to dominate the spirit of a people who were driven from their homes. But joy followed those who had been displaced because of Jesus, and as more and more came to faith in Christ, Saul and his henchmen could not stifle this fruit of the Holy Spirit. That's what you call "living beyond your means". Christians, Jesus expects us to do more than just what we can do on our own. If we only do what we can do on our own, where is the glory for God in that kind of living? We are called to live in a way that brings positive attention to Jesus. With faith and hope, we are called to embody the joy of the Lord as we walk through persecution and opposition. What city will you bring joy to today?

Apostle Meets Huckster

April 4

Read Acts 8:9-13; 2 Cor. 11:12-15; 2 Peter 2:1-3

As Philip preached in Samaria, he ran into a man named Simon. Simon was a guru/charlatan -- a religious huckster. He did magic and sorcery and was quite a celebrity in Samaria. People even said he had the Great Power, and treated him like a god. Simon ate it up, and boasted of his greatness to all who would listen. But when Philip came to town, Simon saw genuine power, and he was attracted. He "believed and was baptized", but for the wrong reasons. He was more interested in the miracles than in the Messiah. Every generation has gurus, shysters, and charlatans, whose followers swoon over their power and charisma. The cash flows in, as people buy their books, diets, and videos. How do you tell the difference between a religious huckster and an apostle? The genuine apostle will never offer you a bag of tricks -- they will offer you a cross.

A Savior for Samaria

April 5

Read Acts 8:14-15, 25; John 4:3-10; 1 Tim. 2:1-4

News of what Philip was doing in Samaria reached Jerusalem, and Peter and John went to see what was happening. It wasn't the miracles that impressed them; it was where the miracles were happening. The Jews looked down on Samaritans and considered them second-class citizens. Along with lepers and harlots, they were the "undesirables", unacceptable to those in good and proper Christian society. They were certainly undeserving of God's grace. But the Holy Spirit was working powerfully among them. The Lord was making it known that Christ is a Savior for all people. God so loved the world! The Lord has not changed His mind. Jesus wants all people "to be saved and come to a knowledge of the truth." Churches that install filters on their front doors (visible or invisible) are not walking in God's will. The gospel is for all people. Find your "Samaria" and go there.

Trying to Buy God

April 6

Read Acts 8:18-24; Micah 3:7-12; 1 Tim. 6:10-11

Simon tried to buy God. He could make a lot of money with the kind of power the apostles had -- and so he offered Peter money for it. Simon had a baptized head, but a worldly heart, and it came close to costing him his life. He tried to buy God, but God is not for sale. What Simon got instead was a dose of prophetic ministry. Peter was not in his "seeker friendly" mode. He called Simon out and told him that his life was in danger. We can make the same mistake as Simon. We can come to God for the "goodies", but fail to give him all our goods. We can have an "experience", but never gain spiritual understanding. Our theology can become skewed. Many believers today study the owner's manual for their car and their big screen TV, more than they study the owner's manual for their soul… the Bible. We need to get back to the basics. Don't try to buy God -- instead, sell out to him.

Right Before God

April 7

Read Acts 8:21-24; Luke 16:13-15

Simon the sorcerer had believed and had been baptized, but his heart was not right before God. He had impure motives as he tried to buy the gift of God. He wanted God's power so that he could be popular and wealthy. Glorifying the Lord had not crossed his mind. Peter chastised Simon, warning him that such disrespect could end in his death. Peter looked into Simon's heart and saw a man who was still captive to his sin, and full of bitterness. This goes to show that we can believe, but still be really messed up in our thinking about God. We can believe, but still have wicked thoughts. We can believe, but still be bitter. We can believe, but still be captive to sin, and ill prepared for ministry. We are saved to bring glory to God. Is that your life's purpose? The self-centered, self-serving disciple is no disciple at all. Beware of Money's power, and work at keeping your heart right before God.

Obedience to the Spirit

April 8

Read Acts 8:26-30; 2 Cor. 9:13; 2 John 1:6

It pays to be obedient to the Spirit of God. Philip was committed to undying obedience, and so when the call came for Philip to go south to a desert road, he went. He didn't know where he would end up, he just went. He didn't know everything that might lie ahead, but he went anyway. That's obedience. And when the call got more specific, (stay near that chariot), that's what Philip did. The angel told Philip to go up to a stranger and stay close. He obeyed, and it changed someone's eternity. We should do the same. Listen for God -- and when God speaks, there's only one correct answer: "Yes". We don't give our children medals for obeying us just 60% of the time! With God, "selective obedience" is an oxymoron. The Lord can do amazing things through us when we obey. Our work can last for eternity when we listen and obey. Souls are at stake. Be obedient to the Spirit.

Lost Believers

April 9

Read Acts 8:27-28, 30-31, 34; James 2:19

God sent Philip to an Ethiopian who worshipped the God of the Jews, but who hadn't met the King of the Jews. He believed in God, but didn't know Christ. He was a "lost believer". Otherwise, God would not have sent Philip. Believing in God does not save people -- only faith in Christ can save people. People can worship God, but not know Jesus. This means that your neighbor, who is surrounded by churches, could be just as lost as that remote tribe in Brazil. It doesn't matter how religious people are -- what matters is if they know Jesus. A lost person is a lost person whether they live in the 10-40 window, or in the house across the street. It doesn't matter if we believe in the God of Moses or worship cows, until we meet Jesus we are all destined for the same godless eternity. That's why God placed Philip on that road to Gaza, and that's why God has you where you are. Share Jesus.

Getting Close Enough to Listen

April 10

Read Acts 8:29-30; John 15:13; Prov. 18:24

God wanted the Ethiopian to hear about Jesus, so he told Philip to stay near the man's chariot. Philip had to get close enough to listen. When he got close, he heard the Ethiopian reading about Jesus from the book of Isaiah. He also heard the questions of the Ethiopian's heart. Philip now had a bridge to share Christ with the man. That could not have happened if Philip hadn't gotten close enough to listen. We have to get close enough to people to listen to them. Too many Christians today are busy answering questions that no one is asking. We spend more time lecturing than listening. We stand at a safe distance and spout directions, when what people need is someone who will draw near to them and listen to their heart. If we're going to be effective at introducing others to the best thing that ever happened in our lives, we will have to get close enough to listen.

A Seeker is Saved

April 11

Read Acts 8:32-38; Romans 10:8-15

As the Ethiopian rode in his chariot, he was reading from the prophet Isaiah, but didn't fully understand it. He asked Philip to explain it, and Philip began with the verses in question and shared the gospel with the Ethiopian. The Ethiopian believed and was baptized, and entered the ranks of those whose names are written in the Book of Life. But it all started with the Scriptures. Christians, we should know how to lead people to Jesus using the Scriptures. The Holy Spirit will put the hunger in their heart, but we should have the knowledge to help them across the line. Philip had obviously studied the Scriptures -- we should too. We have no excuse for not doing so. We have at our fingertips what some have been willing to die for: the Bible. Read it, study it, and use it -- not to condemn people, but to lead seekers to salvation through a knowledge of the Lord Jesus Christ.

Obedience and the Miraculous

April 12

Read Acts 8:39-40; Jeremiah 32:18-20

Obedience is a portal for miracles from God. Philip was obedient and went to a desert road, and the Ethiopian was miraculously converted. Philip was then miraculously transported to another place where he continued his obedient service to God. It's cyclical -- obedience promotes the miraculous, and the miraculous promotes obedience. The one converted was a miracle promoted by obedience. The Ethiopian had traveled a great distance to worship God and was miraculously saved. Don't forget who he was. He was the Secretary of the Treasury for Ethiopia -- a man of prominence. He probably took news of this miracle back to his queen and his nation. Very likely, God used him to spread the gospel throughout Ethiopia. God wants to use believers in the same way today. When we walk in obedience, God can work miracles in us, around us, and through us.

Misdirected Zeal

April 13

Read Acts 9:1-3; Philippians 3:4-6

Saul was one of the most religious men in Israel. He was a Pharisee. He believed in a holy and righteous God -- a God so holy that He would never lower himself to become a man as these "Jesus people" were claiming. Saul's beliefs drove him to try to eradicate this little sect of believers called "The Way", and to stop their gospel from spreading. He oversaw them being beaten up, imprisoned, and even killed. When Saul heard that some of them had fled to Damascus, he put a team of thugs together and headed that way. What Saul didn't know was that he was about to get a wakeup call. In his zeal for God, he had actually become an enemy of God. That can happen to us too. We can become so zealous for our particular brand of faith that we discount, criticize, and fight against others who don't do things like us. Be careful, or like Saul, you can end up fighting against God.

The Damascus Road Experience

April 14

Read Acts 9:3-5; Acts 26:9-15

Saul had been busy beating up on the Bride of Christ, but as he headed down that desert road to Damascus, he met the Groom -- and the Groom was not happy. He knocked Saul to the ground, giving him a taste of his own medicine. Saul had the good sense to address this forceful light as "Lord", asking "Lord, who are you?" His heart skipped a beat, and his breath left him, as he heard a voice say, "I am Jesus, whom you are persecuting." Saul was not only leveled that day, he was humbled. He not only ended up eating dust -- he ended up eating his words. He certainly must have feared for his life. Jesus had Saul's attention, and Saul was now listening. What will it take to get your attention? Will it take a Damascus Road Experience? Will you have to be knocked flat on your back before you look up and finally listen? Maybe today, God is saying to you, "Don't make me come down there." Listen!

Whacked and Commanded

April 15

Read Acts 9:6-7; Luke 9:23-26; James 1:22-25

On the road to Damascus, Jesus whacked Saul upside the head. If that image bothers you, try to come up with a better phrase for being knocked to the ground and made blind. While Christ had Saul's attention, He issued a command: "Go into the city and wait." Saul obeyed. Being knocked down and blinded promotes obedience. Along with all the correct teaching today about the love of Jesus, we must not forget that our Lord has an infinite amount of power. Sometimes God is gentle with us. On other occasions, for reasons known only to Him, He takes a firmer hand. Saul experienced the awesome power of God -- not a gentle breeze or a still small voice, but a whack upside the head from God Almighty. The road to Damascus is never smooth, and it will always humble us. It is populated with proud and stubborn people, who often take some mighty convincing. Never fear -- Jesus is up to the task.

A Familiar Pattern

April 16

Read Acts 9:4-5; Acts 9:8; John 9:24-39

There is a common pattern in the salvation stories of those who come to the Lord later in life. Many, like Saul, start out cursing Jesus and His church. We're blind to God's grace. But then something happens in life. We are knocked to the ground and realize our blindness. As we lay there in the dust of our sin, we have two choices: we can remain face down in the dirt, cursing God; or we can look up, and be open to something different. If we choose the latter, we begin to hear God. Our friends may not hear anything, but we do. It's our time. Jesus is calling our name. We ask, "Who are you?" and realize that it is the Lord. When we hear God, we have another choice -- remain where we are, or get up and do what God says. Saul chose the latter… we should too. Leave that desert road of indecision! Make the walk into your Damascus, and you too can be healed and saved.

Obedience Times Two

April 17

Read Acts 9:10-11; Acts 9:17;
1 Chronicles 21:18-19; Hebrews 11:8-10

One of the things that we can forget as a people saved by grace through faith, is that faith always has an element of obedience in it. Without obedience, we would have very few of the great Bible stories that we know and love. When the Lord told Saul to go to Damascus and wait, Saul obeyed and went. When the Lord told Ananias to go and minister to Saul, Ananias obeyed and went. When God called David to go and build an altar, David obeyed and went. When God told Abraham to go to what would become Israel, Abraham obeyed and went. Because these men were obedient and went where God told them to go, we have all been blessed beyond measure. God can work through even the reluctant disciple, if that disciple will go where they are told to go and do what they are told to do. Will you be that kind of disciple?

Prayer Meeting on Straight Street

April 18

Read Acts 9:8-11; Jonah 2:1-10

After Saul's encounter with Jesus, he went to a house on Straight Street in Damascus. For three days Saul sat in darkness -- the same amount of time Christ spent in the darkness of the tomb. Saul was blind, afraid, and confused; but while he waited there, he prayed. We do not know precisely what Saul prayed, but it was likely a deeply theological and pious prayer like, "Help!" Sometimes that one word prayer is all we can manage in times of deep distress and crisis. Saul knew the Lord was not happy with how he had been living. He didn't know what was going to happen next... perhaps he would even die in Damascus. So in Acts 9:11, Saul prays a "911" prayer. Like Jonah in the belly of the great fish, Saul cried out for mercy. God heard his prayer and sent a deliverer. God still hears "911" prayers. If you are living in darkness today, cry out to the Lord and He will send a deliverer.

Reluctant Disciples

April 19

Read Acts 9:13-14; Ex. 3:10-11; Ex. 4:1, 10-13

The Lord called on Ananias to go and minister to Saul, but Ananias was reluctant. Saul had a nasty reputation in Christian circles. Ananias questioned God and balked at doing what God told him to do. There was danger involved, and he didn't want to go. He sounds a lot like Moses in Exodus. Have you ever argued with Jesus like this? We make excuses. We drag our feet. At times, we flat out refuse. The Lord works with so many reluctant disciples, it's a wonder He doesn't just pull the plug on us all. Most of God's tests do not have multiple choice answers. They are usually "Yes" or "No" questions, and with God, the correct answer is always "Yes". God seldom makes suggestions. Mostly, He issues commands, and when God says "Go", our answer should never be "No". Somebody has to do the hard stuff. On that day it was Ananias. Today it may be you. Say "Yes". Go!

The Scales Come Off

April 20

Read Acts 9:17-19; John 12:35-40

Ananias chose to obey the Lord. He went and laid hands on Saul, and something like scales fell off of Saul's eyes. But scales also came off of Saul's blinded and hardened heart. After this day, Saul never saw Jesus, or the church, in the same way again. He had new eyes, and a new heart. Saul's conversion serves as an example of God's sovereignty, and man's free will. In His sovereignty, the Lord blinded Saul. He was neither the first nor the last to be blinded by our sovereign Lord. But then, because Ananias freely chose to obey God, he became an angel of mercy in Saul's life. Our "angels of mercy" often are flesh and blood people who choose to obey Christ. Ananias chose to minister, and Saul was healed. He was baptized as a new believer, and regained his strength. God's sovereign will and man's free will worked together. The result was an apostle who changed the world.

Chosen Instrument

April 21

Read Acts 9:15; Eph. 1:11-14; 2 Tim. 2:20-21

The Lord chose Ananias to be His instrument to bring healing and salvation to Saul. Christ chose Saul to be His instrument to carry His Name to the Gentiles. God chose Moses to be His instrument to bring deliverance to the Israelites enslaved in Egypt. Ananias, Saul, and Moses were God's chosen instruments for someone, and so are you! If we are in Christ, we are His chosen instruments to bring Him glory, to be His witnesses, to carry His name, and to share His gospel. You may be called to just one person, like Ananias, or you may be called to a nation or people group, like Saul and Moses. But you are Christ's chosen instrument for someone. All that matters is if you perform the function for which you were chosen -- for if you do your job as an instrument of the Lord, someone will likely be in heaven because of your faith and obedient service. And that's what it's all about.

No Christianity Lite

April 22

Read Acts 9:16; Rom. 5:1-4; Rom. 8:17-18; Phil. 3:10-11; Heb. 10:32-36; 1 Peter 4:12-19

There would be no Christianity Lite or Prosperity Gospel for Saul. Right up front, he is informed that he is destined for suffering. His temporary blindness would be the easy part. This suffering would last his entire lifetime. He was hunted down and beaten, stoned within an inch of his life, shipwrecked and stranded at sea, bitten by snakes, and cursed by men. He lived without food or money much of the time, and in the end, the gospel would cost him his very life. We are so into "seeker friendly, sugar coated, what's-in-it-for-me" Christianity today that it's tough for us to believe Jesus would say something like this -- but He did. One wonders how attendance numbers would be affected if every church welcome packet contained this warning. Saul would suffer -- and so will we. If you're not ready for that, you're not ready for the real Jesus.

Keeping the Right Company

April 23

Read Acts 9:19b; 1 Cor. 15:33; 2 Cor. 6:14-17

Saul started off on the right foot in his new Christian life -- he started hanging around with the disciples. The company we keep has an impact on our life. We are influenced by those with whom we choose to associate. One term for this is fellowship. Fellowship is about more than just having fun with Christian friends -- it's about getting close enough to absorb some of Christ's character from those who have walked with Jesus longer than we have. Saul learned about faith, love, hope, mercy, and perseverance from the disciples. His life was enriched by his time with them. Hanging around with mature disciples is important to our spiritual growth. The biblical model of discipleship is not just learning stuff from our teachers, but becoming like them. We become like those we hang around with. Saul chose to hang around with genuine disciples of Jesus. We should do the same.

New Song

April 24

Read Acts 9:20-21; 1 Sam. 10:6; Psa. 40:3

After Saul was healed of his blindness, he immediately began to preach that Jesus is Lord. He had been changed into a different person. God had put a new song in his mouth. People were astonished that this man, who had once arrested Christians as heretics, was now preaching Jesus in synagogues. He sang his new song anywhere people would listen. He had a passion you don't get from reading books about God. Saul's main message in the beginning was his conversion story. He repeated it over and over again to groups and to individuals. He was awestruck at the mercy of God in the face of his sin. Saul preached Jesus with a fervor that could only come from meeting the Lord personally. It doesn't take a seminary degree to preach Jesus -- all it takes is a conversion. Have you been changed by Jesus? Then you have a message. Preach it!

Living It Down

April 25

Read Acts 9:21; Acts 9:26; Proverbs 22:1

A bad reputation is hard to live down. Saul's reputation caused fear instead of faith in the people he went to share his story with. You can't blame them. He had done them harm. It took him a while to live that reputation down. The phrase "live it down", is instructive. We speak about someone "living down" a reputation. The irony is that the reputation we must "live down" was usually obtained from what culture calls "living it up". It can take years to "live it down" after some time of "living it up". We end up being shackled by what we thought was freedom. What we thought would bring happiness, causes despair. Saul had a hard time living down his reputation -- so will we. Be careful about the reputation you are constructing through daily choices. One brick at a time, one day at a time, your reputation is being built. Work at building a reputation you won't have to live down.

Truth That Attracts and Angers

April 26

Read Acts 9:22-23; Acts 9:29; John 8:31-40

The truth about God's grace and mercy began to flow out of Saul, and many were attracted to his message. His passion was contagious, and as his credibility and influence grew, his following increased. Truth is attractive to many people, and yet it angers so many others. There were those who hated Saul and his message enough to try to kill him. Some will just never love the truth. The same thing happened to Jesus, and it can happen to us. When we tell the truth about Christ and His influence in our lives, some will appreciate our words and be drawn to the Lord; but others will despise us and the truth of the gospel. Some will be inspired -- others will conspire. Some will work alongside us -- others will work against us. We have no say in what response we get. It's really none of our business who listens and who doesn't. God will sort that out. Just keep telling the truth.

Fight or Flee

April 27

Read Acts 9:23-25, 9:29-30; 1 Sam. 19:8-12

Sometimes you fight -- sometimes you flee. At times Saul stood his ground… other times he ran for his life. King David did the same. Those with wisdom know whether to fight, or to flee. Only a fool does one or the other, all of the time. Those who flee from every battle, never finding a hill worth dying on, seldom make an impact on this world. But those who never back down, who make every molehill into a mountain worth dying on, seldom last long. Being courageous in the face of overwhelming odds is sometimes the right choice. Retreating so that we can live to fight another day is sometimes an even better choice. Saul fled, because Damascus and Jerusalem were not the hills he was destined to die on. One day he would stand toe to toe with kings and emperors, but not yet. Sometimes you fight -- sometimes you flee. Choose your battles wisely. It's a sign of wisdom.

Good Times - Hard Times

April 28

Read Acts 9:31; Matt. 13:19-23; Heb. 10:32-39

Saul was converted and started preaching. His life was threatened and he fled. And the church grew stronger. Church growth does not always happen just during good times. Hard times can grow us as much as the good times. Life is seldom all good, or all bad. It is mixed together like a stew. We've been led to believe by our ancient foe that hard times mean we are losing. That's not true. If we fold up and bail out every time things get tough, we will never win. Winning armies, winning teams, and winning churches, will endure losses on their pathway to victory. Good times and hard times come together in a package. Persecution is the norm for the faithful church, but so is winning souls in the midst of adversity. Anyone who lives as Christ's disciple will suffer losses. Get over it, and get on with it. We are on our way to winning. The early church thrived in times of great testing -- so can we!

The Advocate

April 29

Read Acts 9:27-28; Job 16:19-21; 1 John 2:1-2

Some wanted nothing to do with this new convert named Saul. They didn't trust him, or want him in their church. But Saul had an advocate in Barnabas. Barnabas got to know Saul. He listened to his heart, and realized that Saul was genuine. So he took the risk of being an advocate for Saul. He stood up for Saul among the church leaders and encouraged them to open their hearts to the miracle of conversion. He called on them to welcome this new face into the church. All of us need an advocate at times -- here on earth, and again when we stand before God. Who will be your advocate when you stand before God? There is only one who has enough influence with the Father to successfully advocate on our behalf. His name is Jesus. He wants to get to know you. He has a heart for you. Do you know Jesus well enough to count on Him as an advocate?

Waiting on the Lord

April 30

Read Acts 9:32-43; Matthew 9:20-22; Luke 13:10-13; John 5:5-9

In this day of instant everything, it is difficult for us to wait. The man Peter healed had been confined to a bed for eight years. The other Scriptures today listed people who had been waiting for healing even longer. But when these verses are preached today, it's usually the instant healing that gets the attention and emphasis. That's what most of us want. We want that moment of healing… but what about the years of waiting? Is that time not also under God's sovereign hand? Is God just sleeping during those times? We must accept the waiting in order to get to the holy moment of healing. We must learn to wait upon the Lord. Suffering while we wait may be one of our most difficult tasks as disciples of Jesus, but there are great things to be learned in the wilderness of pain. Wait upon the Lord. You won't be sorry you did.

Miracle Grow

May 1

Read Acts 9:34-35, 41-42; John 10:25, 37-38

The miracles done by the apostles were done to glorify Christ and grow His Kingdom. When we read in Scripture about someone being healed or raised from the dead, the next thing we usually read is that many people believed and turned to the Lord. Miracles demonstrated the Lordship of Jesus. Today, when we see someone healed on a television ministry, the next thing we usually see is a toll-free number where we can send money, or buy some holy trinket that will heal us too -- if we have enough faith. The disciples did miracles that grew God's Kingdom. Today, miracles are often done to grow someone's bank account. Miracles done in Christ's name should glorify His name. That's something we should remember in this guru-seeking, celebrity-worshipping culture. The miraculous should grow God's Kingdom, not increase someone's bottom line.

Good People Die Every Day

May 2

Read Acts 9:36-39; John 11:23-27, 38-45

Dorcas and Lazarus were kind and generous people who put others ahead of themselves, but they got sick and died. Good people get sick and die every day. Being sick and dying has little to do with how good you are. Many good people got sick and died while Jesus and his disciples walked this earth. Healing and raising the dead were indeed miraculous, but they were not the high water mark of Christ's or Peter's ministries. They were not the end game. There came a day when Dorcas and Lazarus died again, and their decayed bodies await the final resurrection. Their healings were temporary miracles that did not exempt them from eventual death and judgment. The same is true for us. The only lasting miracles are Christ's resurrection and ascension, and His promised return for those who belong to Him. These miracles top them all, and provide our only real hope for eternal life.

Asking for Help

May 3

Read Acts 9:38; Matthew 15:21-22, Matthew 17:14-15; Luke 8:40-42

Tabitha, also known as Dorcas, had some friends who were very wise. When she got sick and died, they appealed to Peter for God's help. It's always good to ask God for help. Why then, is that so hard for us to do? Where did our "I can handle it myself" attitude come from? It starts early in life. We hear kids who are barely three years old saying, "I can do it myself." It is an innate flaw. It is part of our fallen human nature. And it's a killer. It isolates us from others and weakens us. It also denies others the joy of helping us. So we must fight against our tendency to not ask for help. If we don't, we set ourselves up to fail, and eventually, we will even push God out of our lives. Tabitha's friends asked for help. They did the right thing. Be wise and do the same. Learn to ask for help. It will change your life! It may even save your life.

The Power of Prayer

May 4

Read Acts 9:40a; Mark 9:25-29; John 11:41-44

Before Peter did anything for Dorcas, "he got down on his knees and prayed". Before he spouted off to God, or asked God for anything, he prayed. He had learned from Jesus that big miracles require prayer. Resurrection and healing take place where people pray -- really pray. The genesis of healing and resurrection in our lives, and in the lives of those we love, is prayer. Have you prayed for a resurrection in the life of that one you love? We cannot defeat death in this world unless we unleash the hounds of heaven on it. Most of us would say that we want our friends, relatives, and neighbors to be saved. Have you prayed for them today? Prayer calls on the Lord of love and power to intervene where we are powerless. It asks God to do things that we could never do by ourselves. Whether death is physical or spiritual, only the power of God can raise the dead. Pray!

Speaking Words of Life

May 5

Read Acts 9:40b; Luke 7:11-16; John 6:63-68

When Peter confronted death in the house where Tabitha's body had been placed, he prayed first. But then he spoke words of life to her, telling her to rise up. Prayer should come first, but at some point we are called to speak words of life into those around us. Words of life can be as simple as telling the story of what Jesus has done for you. They can be spoken when we ask another if we can pray for them. They can be shared when we explain the gospel to someone and ask if they would like to receive Jesus. Prayer is a great calling and should never be forsaken, but speaking words of life is of equal importance. One should not replace the other -- they work in tandem. When we fail to speak the words of life, we deny our full calling, and foolishly attempt to defeat the enemy with one hand tied behind our back. Pray, and speak the words of life into those dying around you.

Hands On Ministry

May 6

Read Acts 9:41a; Mark 8:22-25; Luke 13:10-13

Praying and speaking words of life are important, but one more thing is often called for in ministry. At some point we are all called to take another's hand and help them to their feet. If our ministry is indeed a ministry of Christ, it will often become a "hands on" ministry. We are called to intercede in prayer, to speak the words of life, and sometimes to become the hands of Jesus here on Earth. We embrace that grieving parent. We cuddle that child who is in pain. We reach down and offer a hand to those who have fallen. We lay our hands on the sick and ask for their healing. We hold the hands of those who walk through the valley of the shadow of death. We are called to be the healing, holding, and helping hands of Jesus in a world filled with desperate, destitute, and dying people. Never underestimate the power of a touch from Jesus. Reach out and use your hands for God's glory.

Giving the Miracle a Voice

May 7

Read Acts 9:41-42; 1 Thess. 5:19; Psalm 96:3

Miracles were not meant to be kept secret. They are granted to glorify God. For that reason, at some point we should give the miracle a voice. When someone repents and turns to Christ, spiritually they have been raised from the dead. The best thing we can do for them after that is to lead them to tell someone. We present them to others alive. Peter did this with Dorcas. He took her out in public and presented her alive to the people. Peter gave the miracle a voice. Jesus does miracles today. Some of those miracles are reading this page right now. Give those miracles a voice. It's sad that so many of God's miracles never see the light of day because they are never declared. Thus, they fail to accomplish God's purpose of glorifying his Son, and the power of the Holy Spirit is quenched by human reluctance. Proclaim the victory. Souls are at stake. Give the miracle a voice.

Hospitality

May 8

Read Acts 9:43; Rom. 12:13, 16:23; 1 Peter 4:8-9

It would be easy to skip over Acts 9:43 as an insignificant addition to a miraculous story of healing and resurrection. But it's an important detail. It highlights the hospitality of a common working man named Simon. He was a tanner, and probably good at his trade, but he is not immortalized for excelling at his craft. He is known because he hosted Peter for "some time". The early apostles depended on hospitality wherever they traveled. The gospel was not a money-making business, and they had no "travel benefits". It is safe to say that the gospel would not have prospered like it did in those early days had there not been people willing to host those who were fearlessly preaching. Common everyday people, most of them nameless, helped propel the name of Jesus onto the world stage, by sacrificing to practice hospitality. Take a moment today and thank God for their work.

Religious, But Not Related

May 9

Read Acts 10:1-5; Matt. 8:5-13; Eph. 2:8-9

Cornelius, a Centurion in the Roman army, was a good man. He was devout and religious, and he had gotten God's attention because of his generosity and compassion. But he still lacked one vital thing -- he did not yet know Jesus. He was religious, but not yet related. God wanted to see him receive eternal life, but in spite of all his goodness, the Centurion was not ready to face God. He needed more than goodness and religion. The same is true for us. We need more than religion, kindness, generosity, and compassion. We need a personal relationship with Jesus Christ. We can be a good person, go to church, be generous, and treat others with compassion, but we can still die lost if we have never really met the Savior and become a disciple of the Lord Jesus. As we will see, God sent Peter to Cornelius, and Cornelius believed the gospel. We would be wise to do the same.

Our Memorial Offering to God

May 10

Read Acts 10:3-4; 2 Cor. 9:6-9; Rev. 5:6-8

The wise Christian thinks of eternity daily, for we live with one foot on Earth and the other in Heaven. We consider our earthly legacy, but more importantly, we are mindful of our eternal legacy. We consider what is of worth in God's sight and how God will remember us. Scripture lists at least two things that constitute the kind of memorial noticed by God -- our prayers and our giving to the poor. The time we spend with God because of our love for Him, and what we give away to help others, are like putting our best foot forward into heaven. God noticed these two things about Cornelius. When done with the right heart today, these two things still rise like incense to Heaven as a pleasing aroma before the Lord. How are you doing in these two areas? Do you pray because you love God? Is your giving to the poor memorable? Intimate prayer and generous giving still please God.

Obedience to the Vision

May 11

Read Acts 10:3, 5-8; Acts 16:9-10

Cornelius had a very specific vision. He was to send some men to bring Peter to his house. He obeyed the vision, but if he had complied with the customs of his day, he would never have done so. Roman Centurions did not usually invite Jews into their homes. The Romans had conquered the Jews and considered them a weird and strange people. But Cornelius was obedient to the vision, and it changed the history of the church. Paul also had a vision about going to Macedonia. He too obeyed, and once again, history was changed. Obedience to the vision God gives us is crucial to the Kingdom of God. You don't have to be a mystic to receive vision -- just read the Bible. God's word can speak plenty of vision into our lives today. We can receive direction from God on a daily basis. Will you be obedient to the vision God gives to you? If so, you could be involved in changing history.

Double Vision

May 12

Read Acts 10:9-17; Acts 26:19-23

Soon after Cornelius received a vision from the Lord, Peter received his own vision. It was a case of "double vision". Peter was to begin to consider as "clean" anything that God had made "clean". He would soon discover that this included people as well as food. Just to be sure Peter got the message, God repeated it three times. Like Cornelius, Peter was obedient to his vision and took the gospel to the house of a despised Roman Gentile. Later Paul the apostle would also receive a vision to take the gospel to the Gentiles. Jesus has died for the sins of the world, not just for the Jews. All of these men obeyed their visions and took action. They went where God told them to go at great risk to themselves. Their obedience is why we have the Church today. Have you been obedient to the vision God has given you? He sends us to those who need to hear the truth. Obey and go!

God's Thing is New Things

May 13

Read Acts 10:11-16; Isaiah 43:19; Rev. 21:5

God's thing is new things. We crave consistency -- God is continuously making things new. It is His prerogative -- He is sovereign. Who are we to dispute His desire, or His object of change? God had been clear about clean and unclean foods, but in a vision He told Peter that this was changing. Peter could now eat foods that were previously forbidden. The vision was a preview of the new concept that God's ultimate food, Jesus, the Bread of Life, was to be available to everyone, even those who had been formerly declared unclean. The Roman Centurion and all other Gentiles were declared worthy of God's grace. God does not change, but the practices of His people can change. The church tends to enshrine practices and close their eyes to new vision. It should be the other way around. The Lord can do a new thing whenever He wants. Let's make sure we don't get in His way.

No Coincidence

May 14

Read Acts 10:17-21; Habakkuk 2:3; Proverbs 19:21; Romans 8:28

The word coincidence is not in God's vocabulary. It was no coincidence that Peter's vision of unclean animals immediately preceded a visit from some "unclean" Gentile servants of Cornelius. Peter decided that the timing of these events was not a coincidence. When dealing with "God stuff", pay attention to timing. God may send us messages in multiple forms. When the Lord wants to move us, He often uses more than one vehicle. Pay attention to the timing of events in your life. Sometimes, multiple people will give us the same message. Sometimes, what we perceive as a negative event takes us to a new place in our life, and when we arrive we realize that it was a "God thing". Sometimes, when doors close, others can open at almost the same time. Pay attention to timing -- that series of coincidences may not be coincidental at all.

Servant Hearts

May 15

Read Acts 10:22-23; Col. 1:3-7; Titus 1:1; James 1:1; 2 Peter 1:1; Jude 1:1

The Church of Jesus Christ would not have grown without those who had a heart to serve the King of kings. People with a servant's heart went to get Peter for Cornelius. People with a servant's heart went with Peter to the house of Cornelius. Paul, James Peter, and Jude preached the gospel, discipled new believers, and wrote letters to the churches that have survived to this day… because they had servant's hearts. Their pay was minimal -- their investment was huge. They and millions of nameless servants down through the ages endured hardships, faced danger, and sacrificed their lives so that we could have a knowledge of the Lord Jesus Christ. We are called to pass it on. "Non-serving Christian" is an oxymoron. How are you serving the Lord? In big ways and small ways, find some way to serve the Lord today.

Taking Risks for the Gospel

May 16

Read Acts 10:23; Acts 10:28; 2 Cor. 11:24-28

Peter took a great risk by letting Gentiles stay in his home. He took another great risk by going to Cornelius's house to visit him. It was against Jewish law. Jews were not to enter the houses of Gentiles, let alone stay the night. Christians violating Jewish law were already being killed. Peter could have easily been next. Spiritually and politically, the Romans were despised and hated in Israel. They were usually polytheistic, and were considered unclean. Peter was contaminating and condemning himself by going there, but he took the risk. If we are going to be obedient to our calling, and take the gospel with us wherever we go, we are going to have to take some risks. To save lives, we must often risk our own. If we refuse to take risks for the gospel, we are doomed to be sterile believers. We cannot fulfill the commission Christ gave us unless we are willing to take some risks. Will you do that?

Relatives and Friends

May 17

Read Acts 10:24; Mark 5:18-20; John 1:40-42

When Cornelius found out that Peter was coming to his house, he didn't try to keep it from his friends and neighbors. He put out a press release, put up posters, and phoned everyone he knew. Well, not really, but he did call together his close friends and relatives. Today we have believers who barely mention their church in conversation with friends and relatives. They don't want to offend anyone. They act as though they were ashamed of Jesus and the church. They keep their faith and the good news to themselves. Not Cornelius! He put the word out. If there had been radio in his day, there would probably have been a commercial with "BE THERE!" at the end. We laugh, but if the gospel really is for everyone, why don't we act like it? If the message of Jesus really is life changing stuff, why wouldn't we want to expose our friends and neighbors to it in any way we can?

Star Gazing

May 18

Read Acts 10:25-26, Acts 14:8-18; Romans 12:2-3

Cornelius wanted to treat Peter like a celebrity. Peter would have none of it. It would have been easy for him to exploit having walked with Jesus. He had been given power to heal the sick and raise the dead. That can certainly be heady stuff. Instead Peter saw himself as just another one of God's many servants. He was a model of godly humility. Some Christian leaders today have forgotten this apostolic lesson. They spend more time basking in the spotlight, than walking in God's light. They are encouraged by the fawning celebrity worship of groupie Christians. We flock to where the biggest crowds are. We covet the fame, hoping that some of it will rub off on us if we can just get near enough. We need to get back to humility again. There is only one Messiah, and we all serve under Him. Let's be done with the hero worship. Let's stoop to wash feet, more than we seek to gaze at stars.

No Favorites

May 19

Read Acts 10:33-35, 44-48; James 2:1-10

Peter received God's message. God does not show favoritism. The gospel was not just for the Jew, nor was it just for the rich and significant people of the world. The gospel is for everyone. God accepts those who seek Him from every nation and from every walk of life. If Christ does not show favoritism, the Church, the Bride of Christ, should not be found showing favoritism. Unfortunately, that is not always the case. When God looks at people, He sees the soul. He does not see skin color, national origin, or income level. He doesn't see suits and ties, or sandals and t-shirts. We should not be found doing so in our churches. It should not surprise us when the Spirit and blessing of God falls upon those who don't look like they belong. The gospel is for everyone. Even you! Jesus died for the sins of the world. Even yours! The gospel is for all who will receive it. God does not show favoritism.

Chosen Witnesses

May 20

Read Acts 10:36-41; Acts 1:8; Acts 2:32

Peter thought of himself as a chosen witness. He knew the truth about Jesus, and he was called to share it with others. We who believe today also have a witness, and we have the same calling as Peter to share it. You are a chosen witness. Is that how you see yourself? Part of our witness is the truth about Jesus. Every Christian should know the simple gospel and how to share it. It is unchanging and eternal, but is adaptable to any situation or culture. The other part of our witness is what we have seen, and what Jesus has done in our life. We all have a story of some kind. This part of our story grows and changes. It's different this year than last year. There is someone who needs to hear your story and witness. As we said yesterday, the gospel is for everyone, and so is the story God has given you. You are His chosen witness!

Commanded to Preach and Testify

May 21

Read Acts 10:42-43; 2 Timothy 1:8-12, 4:2-5

The reason Peter risked going to the house of Cornelius is that he had been commanded to preach and testify. He had been commanded to speak about the Lord Jesus. He was obedient to the command. The command has not changed. It is a command for all time, to all disciples. Just before Christ ascended, He commanded His disciples to preach and to testify. The command extends out in time to those who follow Him today. We are His disciples, and that makes us His witnesses and preachers. We have been commanded to testify to His grace and mercy. We have been commanded to preach the gospel of Christ's love -- to speak of His death on the cross for our sin, and of His resurrection. It is a message of eternal hope with Jesus as Lord and Savior, but of eternal judgment without Him. The gospel is for everyone, and the command to preach and testify is for all disciples.

Basic Gospel 101

May 22

Read Acts 10:39-43; Luke 24:44-48

The gospel is an amazing gift from God, and we are commanded to share it. It's not complicated, and its presentation does not have to be perfect. The Holy Spirit does the calling, the persuading, and the saving. Our part is witnessing to its reality in our lives and declaring it. God created us to be in relationship with Him, but we have all sinned and gone our own way. Knowing we were lost, God came to Earth in Jesus as a sacrifice for our sins. He was crucified. He died and was buried, but God raised Him from the dead and many saw Him. Christ's death paid the penalty for our sin. His resurrection proved that God accepted His payment. Everyone who believes and accepts His grace and mercy can receive forgiveness of sins through his name and be saved. Jesus is alive, and we are saved through our relationship with Him. Do you believe this? It's a yes or no answer.

Eating with Sinners

May 23

Read Acts 11:1-3; Mark 2:15-17

Peter experienced a great spiritual breakthrough at the house of Cornelius. God had opened the door of salvation to the Gentiles. But when Peter got home, he faced the scrutiny of the religious community because he had gone to the home of "sinners" and ate with them. Instead of being thrilled that lost people had come to Christ, these nitpickers were offended that Peter went to them in the first place. Peter's consolation was that they had said the same thing about Jesus. Jesus received the same criticism for going where the "sinners" were and ministering to them. He even once said that they were why he came into the world -- He came to save sinners. If God calls us, we should not refuse to minister to those that religionists consider "unclean". Be certain it is the call of God and not of your flesh, but wherever God sends us, we go. We set a guard upon our hearts and we go.

Sharing Our Story

May 24

Read Acts 11:4-15

When Peter retold the story of his vision from heaven, the Bible says he did so "precisely". He took pains to describe it accurately. Peter likely retold his story many times in his life. Likewise, the story of Paul is told three different times in the book of Acts. Surely he told it many times. When there is a great story, it gets retold again and again. Peter's vision and Paul's conversion were acts of God that shaped the direction of the infant church, and broadened the horizons of Christianity. Our stories are much the same. They may not be as dramatic, but they are no less important. Every true story of God's grace broadens the horizons of Christianity and helps shape the ongoing narrative of the church. Do not hesitate to share your story. There is no need to exaggerate it or embellish it. It has the power to change lives just as it is. Share it often, and share it precisely. God will do the rest.

Opposing God

May 25

Read Acts 11:16-17; Heb. 11:7; Jonah 1:1-3

When God calls us to go somewhere, and do something for him and we refuse, we end up opposing God. When Jonah refused to go to Nineveh, he was opposing God. If Noah had declined to build an ark, he would have been opposing God. And if Peter had not obeyed the vision and gone to the household of Cornelius, he would have been opposing God. Today, when we will not go where the Lord tells us to go, or do what He calls us to do we also end up opposing God. How foolish can we be? Each one of us has some kind of calling on our life that could reach a household somewhere for Jesus. Maybe it's a household across the sea. Maybe it's the household across the street. Maybe it's even our own household. Go where the Spirit tells you to go, and do what He calls you to do, or join the ranks of those opposing God.

Repentance Unto Life

May 26

Read Acts 11:18; 2 Cor. 7:10; Isa. 30:15

The early church soon concluded that even Gentiles had been granted the opportunity to repent and receive new life in Jesus. What does it mean to be granted repentance unto life? It is the combination of God's sovereign grace and our free will. First, it is a grant. We do not have to pay it back. We cannot pay it back. We have been granted salvation. It is by grace we have been saved. But the grant is for an opportunity. We have been given the opportunity to choose -- to believe in faith that Jesus saves. We can receive God's gift, or refuse it. We can repent and receive eternal life, or we can decline God's offer and continue to live in the darkness of death. Repentance unto life means choosing to let God change our life. We abandon our old destructive behavior, and embrace new life-giving behaviors. We are born again into a new life with Christ. Have you repented unto life?

Thinking Outside the Box

May 27

Read Acts 11:7-12; Isaiah 43:19

God often calls us to do things that we wouldn't ordinarily do, in ways we've never done it before. This is what happened to Peter. One phrase we use today to express this concept is "thinking outside the box". In Peter's vision, the Lord called him to think outside the box. God was doing a new thing! The church would need to greatly expand its box. Today, many churches have a box that everyone is expected to fit into, and woe to the person who thinks outside of that particular box. But many people that Jesus wants to save do not fit in the average church's box. It must grieve the Holy Spirit that while Jesus is building a mansion in glory, His church seems to be consumed with box- making. And while God's people strain to maintain their precious little boxes, Jesus comes along and says, "Your boxes are way too small." In these last days, it's time to think outside the box.

Earning the Title

May 28

Read Acts 11:26; Acts 26:28; 1 Peter 4:16

As the news about Jesus spread, more and more Gentiles came to faith. In Antioch, Jesus changed some new believers in such a profound way that their faith became legendary. They impressed folks around them so much that they earned a radical new title. People began to call them Christians. They were so different, so much like Jesus, that they were labeled with His name. A new brand name was born in Antioch. At first, the label was derogatory. It was a slur. Antagonists and persecutors used the name to stereotype and ridicule the church. They were seen as a very weird bunch and looked down upon by the intellectuals of their day. The label stuck, and over time it became something of which to be proud. The name that began as a slur became a badge of honor. It became a title to strive for -- a title earned by wholeheartedly living for Jesus. Go for the title! Live for Jesus.

Sent Out By Force

May 29

Read Acts 11:19; Acts 8:1-4

It wasn't always a mystical missionary spirit that carried the name of Jesus abroad. The seeds of the gospel were often spread by the winds of persecution. But as people fled from the death threats and the beatings, they continued to share the gospel story. What was designed to silence the message of Christ ended up amplifying it to the point that it became unstoppable. God took what was intended for evil, and used it for good. Sometimes the pain, suffering, and persecution of this life produce the sweetest fruit for the kingdom of God. Trials and troubles often force us out of our comfort zones and into situations where our lights can shine brightly. We can be pushed into doing heroic things that we would not have ordinarily done, and taken to places where the name of Christ has not yet been spoken. Wherever life takes you, share Jesus.

Good News for Everyone

May 30

Read Acts 11:20; Rom. 1:16-17; Rom. 10:11-13

Not everyone scattered by persecution shared the good news. Some shared only with those who were just like them. But others told the gospel to non-Jewish people. They shared the good news with everyone, and many Greeks in Antioch came to faith in Christ. The church opened its doors to those who had previously been excluded, and they came in. We honor God by sharing our faith with everyone around us. Ask the Spirit to free your muted tongue. Tell your story to everyone who will listen. Stop trying to be like everyone else and start being who you've been called to be. Stop trying to be liked by everyone and begin loving others enough to tell them the truth. Open your church to those who wouldn't be welcomed in other places. Share the gospel with those that others consider undesirable. That's what the castaway Christians did in Antioch. We can do the same.

Where the Rubber Meets the Road

May 31

Read Acts 11:21; Luke 1:65-66; Ezekiel 1:3

Being a Christian is a bit like being a tire on a car. When the Lord's hand is with us, we are on the move, but every time we move, some of the tire's surface is worn off. The only way for the tread to remain fully intact is to never move the vehicle. But we can't go anywhere unless the tires turn. Unless we're willing to accept some wear and tear and to experience some tread loss, we will never fulfill our purpose, which is to move our gospel vehicle down the road. Even if tires just sit on the shelf and never touch the ground, the rubber eventually ages and gets weak. So if we just sit around and never take our faith to the place where the rubber meets the road, we will die of old age, never having been used for the purpose God intended. When God's hand is on us, we will be moving. Submit to the wear and tear of the road, and if God's hand is with us, we will be restored as we move along.

Making News for Jesus

June 1

Read Acts 11:22; Matt. 4:24; Luke 7:15-17

Good news travels slower than bad news, but it does travel. When faith is genuine, it becomes newsworthy. If we love consistently, we make news for Jesus that goes beyond the token church page in the local newspaper. If the only news we generate is soup suppers, car washes, pancake feeds, and Vacation Bible Schools, we haven't really done much for Jesus. If the only time people know we belong to a church is when they read our obituary in the newspaper, we have failed our calling. Live a life that produces good news -- news that reaches the ears of unbelievers and skeptics. Surprise the world with love, grace, compassion, and generosity. Show your neighbors who Jesus is with your life. Use every opportunity God provides to speak of the changes Christ has brought to your life. When the church does this, the label "Christian" will become admirable again.

Evidence of Grace

June 2

Read Acts 11:23; Acts 26:20; 1 Cor. 4:1-2

When Barnabas looked at the lives of the new Christians at Antioch, he saw evidence of God's grace. They were becoming a reflection of Jesus. The evidence of grace is a changed life -- a life that causes others to say, "There's something different about you. What is it?" The change starts when we believe the truth about Jesus. This lights a fire, and the grace of God begins to percolate in us. As we feed on God's word and spend time with God in prayer, the way we live begins to change, and we begin to produce the evidence of grace. If we see salvation as just a momentary decision that supplies us with a "get out of hell free" card, this likely won't happen. God calls us to more than just a day of salvation. He calls us to a lifetime of discipleship. As the evidence of grace grows in our lives, others will be drawn to the glow of the gospel. Is your life producing evidence of grace?

Full of It

June 3

Read Acts 11:24; Acts 6:8; John 1:14; Luke 11:39

You may have heard the expression, "He's full of it." It is not usually meant as a compliment. When Luke speaks of Barnabas being sent to Antioch, he tells us that Barnabas was a man "full of the Holy Spirit and faith." When John speaks of Jesus, he describes the Lord as "full of grace and truth." Stephen, the church's first recorded martyr, is described as "a man full of grace and power." Conversely, Jesus described the Pharisees as "full of greed and wickedness." How would God describe you? If the Lord described you as "full of it", what would he be talking about? What a glorious epitaph for our tombstones, if it could honestly be said of us, "He (she) was a good man (woman), full of the Holy Spirit and faith, and he (she) brought a great number of people to the Lord." If we're going to be described as being full of something, let's work at making it "the Holy Spirit and faith."

Teachable Disciples

June 4

Read Acts 11:25-26; Acts 18:11; Mark 6:34

One of the traits that marked the early disciples and earned them the label "Christian" was their teachability. Like sponges, the believers in Antioch soaked up the teaching of Saul and Barnabas for a whole year. With diligence and determination, they sacrificed their time to learn. Today, many who identify as Christians have lost that spirit. Far too many are just "Sunday morning Christians". They seldom read the Bible for themselves, study Scripture together, or spend time in prayer. Becoming a mature disciple does not happen automatically. There is no magic pill. It takes discipline, and requires a teachable spirit, which is a choice. One of the greatest weaknesses of the church today is the lack of teachable disciples. Apathy, busyness, indifference, and arrogance define many believers, and these attitudes hinder discipleship. Don't be one of the unteachables.

Christian = Generous

June 5

Read Acts 11:27-30; 2 Cor. 8:1-7; 2 Cor. 9:12-15

The believers in Antioch, derisively labeled as "Christians" because of their faith in a risen Lord, demonstrated what it means to follow Jesus. They not only supported one another in times of need, they modeled generous giving, sending money to help people they didn't even know. This is what happens when self-preservation ceases to be our goal in life. It happens when we get outside ourselves -- our wants and our needs. It happens when we see that what we have is a gift from God, given to us to share with others. It happens when we have faith that God will take care of us even when we give our stuff away. These people were not wealthy by the world's standards, but they were rich in grace and mercy, and they became a legend in their own time. They earned the name "Christian" -- a curse word that eventually evolved into a badge of honor. Are you growing into the name?

No Guarantee of Safety

June 6

Read Acts 12:1-4; Luke 14:25-33; Luke 21:10-19

Righteousness is no guarantee of safety. James was arrested and quickly executed by Herod for his faith. Peter appeared headed for the same fate. The disciples had no guarantee of safety. Thousands of believers in the book of Acts shared the gospel at the risk of their lives. Obedience, not personal safety, was the primary concern of the disciples. When Jesus said you must lay down your life for the gospel, He meant it. Today, many Christians want a guarantee of safety before they step out in faith. Forget about our lives, we are reluctant to sacrifice even our popularity. We must abandon the false teaching that our prosperity and popularity are God's number one concern. Lost souls are His chief concern. He gave the life of his Son for them. Do we really think our lives are more important than that? Being a disciple has no guarantee of safety. Be a disciple anyway.

Earnest Prayer

June 7

Read Acts12:5; James 5:16; Psa. 107:28-30

If one takes enough Scripture out of context, they can come up with a guaranteed formula for achieving answered prayer. Prayer is often taught as if it were a matter of pushing the right buttons; after which God is obligated to grant our requests. This is a distorted picture of prayer. There is no guaranteed formula, but God does point to earnestness as a factor in powerful prayer. The church was praying earnestly for Peter, and God sent an angel to set him free. Does that mean that the church was less earnest in their prayers for James? No! God answers prayer in His way, in His time, and for His glory. We pray because God tells us to pray, and we want to be obedient. We pray because it makes a difference. There are too many great personal testimonies that point to the power of prayer for us to ignore. Never underestimate the power of earnest prayer.

God's Intervention

June 8

Read Acts 12:6-11; Job 1:18-22

God is sovereign, and sometimes chooses to interject Himself into human history. James was killed by Herod, but Peter was spared by an angelic visitation. We may question God's fairness and sit in judgment of Him, but we do not view history from eternity. Why do we make deliverance from physical death the measuring stick of God's power and love? Is personal survival really the only definition of God's mercy? Is life here on earth really better than eternity in heaven? When we say at funerals, "They're in a better place"… do we not really mean it? Perhaps James, not Peter, received the greater miracle here. When God intervenes and we survive, we should praise Him -- and when God doesn't appear to come through, we should praise Him. God is sovereign, and we who believe are blessed, whether the angel comes to save us, or to take us home.

Doubting God's Miracles

June 9

Read Acts 12:11-16; Matthew 14:25-31

The church was praying for Peter's deliverance, but when God answered their prayers, they doubted and were astonished that he showed up at their door. They were surprised by God's miracle. We should never doubt God's ability to do miracles. Our God can provide astonishing answers to prayer. However, we must be careful how we define the word "miracle". Things don't have to go our way for miracles to occur. They can happen, even when we don't get what we want. We must abandon our self-centered approach to the miraculous. Miracles often go far beyond the limited scope of our personal benefit. An examination of Scripture will show that God's miracles do not always include our personal well-being, or the well-being of those we love. Never doubt the ability of God to do miracles! Just be sure you don't define "miracle" so narrowly that God cannot succeed.

Eaten By Worms

June 10

Read Acts 12:18-23; Acts 14:8-18

The main difference between the disciples and Herod was who they sought to glorify with their lives. The disciples sought to glorify God. Herod sought to glorify himself. But God's patience with Herod finally ran out. When the people praised Herod as a god, instead of correcting them, he accepted it and soaked it up. For his sin, he was struck down and "eaten by worms". Herod thought of himself as a god, and it cost him his life. It still costs us our lives when we think of ourselves as gods. We mock God when we serve ourselves rather than the Lord -- when we are absorbed with self-glorification rather than glorifying Christ. We walk with Herod when we advance ourselves rather than advancing the gospel. We worship ourselves when we rationalize our sin and excuse behavior that is offensive to the God of Heaven. This is the basic flaw of humanity. Never fail to give glory to God.

God's Sovereignty - Our Free Will

June 11

Read Acts 12:24; Isaiah 49:22; Isaiah 30:15

God is sovereign, and all the Herods, Hitlers, and Ayatollahs of this world will never stop the steady march of the gospel through time. It will continue to "increase and spread" in the best of times, and in the worst of times. Today, you are either a miracle of God, or a miracle in waiting. We are carried to Christ on the shoulders of those who give their lives to glorify God. That mother or grandmother who prayed helped beckon you. That friend or neighbor who shared Jesus and invited you to church lifted the banner. But although God is sovereign, in this lifetime we have choices. God allows us to choose Him or reject Him. We have free will. Salvation is in Christ, repentance, and resting in faith, but many will have none of it. God is sovereign, but lets us choose. What will you choose? Will you be among those who have none of it, or among those who trust in the Lord?

Labeled a Quitter

June 12

Read Acts 12:25; Acts 13:13; Acts 15:36-40; Colossians 4:10; 2 Timothy 4:11

John Mark had some ups and downs in his ministry. He eventually wrote the Gospel of Mark, but not before he was labeled a "quitter" and caused a deep disagreement between Paul and Barnabas. They took Mark on a missionary journey, but he left the team and went back home. When Barnabas wanted to take Mark on a subsequent trip, Paul said no. He saw Mark as unreliable. They disagreed so strongly that they parted ways. But later in Paul's letters, we see that Mark once again became a trusted companion. Most of us go through times in our faith when we fail to follow through or complete our mission. All of Christ's disciples failed Him at some point. But with Jesus, failure is never final -- the "quitter" label need not stick forever. Our God is a God of second chances. Accept His offer of grace and get back in the game.

Gifted Prophets and Teachers

June 13

Read Acts 13:1; Romans 12:4-8

The church at Antioch was blessed with gifted prophets and teachers. Among them were Barnabas and Saul. The Holy Spirit had gifted them to preach the word and teach the great truths of Jesus. These gifts of the Spirit helped them grow the church in Antioch, and qualified them to be the first formally commissioned missionaries. The church at Antioch eventually sent Saul and Barnabas out to evangelize and plant churches in other places. Those with prophetic gifting speak the truth of God boldly into their cultures, even when that truth is difficult. Prophetic teaching is not always positive. It disturbs our peace, and calls us to change. But prophets preach and teach God's word regardless of the consequences. You too have been given a gift to use for Christ's glory -- perhaps even more than one. Discover it, and use it to grow God's Kingdom.

Set Apart and Called

June 14

Read Acts 13:2; Romans 1:1-4

Saul and Barnabas were "set apart" and "called" by God. Is this still important? Many churches today look for a leader with a higher education, rather than a leader with a higher calling. Too many see ministry as a profession rather than a calling. To be truly effective for God's Kingdom, a call is essential. Without a calling, we may become good employees of a church, but seldom excel as great servants of Jesus Christ. Without a calling, we are doomed to being duty-bound workers rather than Spirit-filled laborers. Without a calling, we will lack the stamina and zeal necessary to complete the difficult missions set before us. Barnabas and Saul would need that sense of calling to carry them through lonely nights when they'd been rejected, beaten, and jailed for disturbing the peace. Being called and set apart would keep them going when others were giving up. It still works that way.

Called, Affirmed, Sent Out

June 15

Read Acts 13:3; Luke 9:1-2; John 17:13-18

There is a sense in which all who follow Jesus are "sent". The call to "go and make disciples" in Matthew 28, and the call "be my witnesses" in Acts 1, are standing orders for all who believe that Jesus is Lord. All Christians have been "sent" in some way, to someone, somewhere. But the Holy Spirit led the church in Antioch to bless Saul and Barnabas for a special mission. They were sent out as traveling evangelists and church planters. They were called, affirmed and sent out by a local church just like yours and mine. God's blessing came through the church where they were serving. Today, we have too many "lone rangers" who see gifts in themselves and call themselves. They seek counsel from no one, and have little, if any accountability. But the pattern set by the early church is for those who feel a call to seek the counsel and blessing of their church. That's still a good plan.

Proclamation

June 16

Read Acts 13:4-5; John 12:32; Colossians 1:25-29; 1 John 1:1-3

When Saul and Barnabas arrived at Salamis, their mission's purpose immediately became clear. They had come to proclaim the word of God. They preached the good news of Christ's life, death, and resurrection for the salvation of all who would repent and believe. As individuals and churches, we may use various methods to share the love of Jesus, and point people to the Lord… feeding programs, big events, great music, or children's programs. We find ways to love people and give glory to God, but our highest calling is to share the gospel -- to proclaim the word of God. If we fail at this, we have failed our mission. Whatever it takes, we must proclaim it. We tell people about Jesus. We don't save people -- only Jesus does that. But we lift Him up, because if we lift Him up, He will draw people unto himself. That's our calling.

Training the Next Generation

June 17

Read Acts 13:5b; Deut. 6:6-7; Judges 2:10

When Saul and Barnabas set off on their first missionary journey, they took a young man by the name of John Mark with them as an intern. Their ministry team was intergenerational. Saul later did the same thing with Timothy. He was always training up someone younger. We should also be training up the next generation, and whether we know it or not, we already are. We all have a John Mark of some kind watching us - - a teen, or a child, or a grandchild. As they follow you around today and observe your walk, will they be inspired to follow Jesus? Who will be serving the Lord in the next generation because you modeled faith for them and made a difference in their lives? Someone has said that the church is always only one generation away from extinction. Do your part to prevent that from happening. Make disciples in the generations that follow in your footsteps.

The Intelligent Man

June 18

Read Acts 13:6-7; 1 Cor. 1:18-25

After sailing to the island of Cyprus, Saul and Barnabas preached in the city of Salamis. Then they traveled to Paphos where they met a sorcerer and a seeker. The sorcerer was a Jewish false prophet named Bar-Jesus Elymas. The seeker's name was Sergius Paulus. He was a proconsul, which means he was a man of power. Luke describes him as an intelligent man who invited Saul and Barnabas to his house because he wanted to hear the word of God. Truly intelligent people still want to hear the word of God. Christianity is often derided as a religion for the gullible and the unsophisticated, but the opposite is really true. Intelligence and seeking God go together. One could even say that the essence of true intelligence is seeking God. The traditional Christmas time phrase, "Wise Men Still Seek Him", is an intelligent statement year round.

Blinded By Darkness

June 19

Read Acts 13:9-11; John 3:18-21; Matt. 15:14

Not only are there prophets and teachers in the church, there are also false prophets and teachers. Elymas was one of those false teachers. He was a sorcerer who tried to turn the proconsul away from believing in Christ. But Paul would have none of it, and confronted the powers of darkness. He silenced Elymas by calling down blindness upon him. The voice of darkness was silenced by being blinded. The mouth seldom boasts of what the eyes cannot see. False prophets operate in the spirit of darkness, and turn people away from the light of Jesus. They emit an aura of wisdom, but they are blind guides who end up groping and stumbling in the darkness. Do not join them in their blindness. Confront them when you find them. They will put up a fight, but never forget, the Spirit of the Lord is stronger. No sorcery can defeat the power of God. Take the fight to them.

Name Change

June 20

Read Acts 13:9; Acts 13:13; Phil. 2:4-7

In Acts 13:9, a name change occurs. From now on, we no longer read of Saul. He has become Paul. We have seen this before in Scripture, and it usually has significance. In those days, names had meaning that often reflected the personality of the one bearing the name. Saul was born a Jew and given a Hebrew name by his parents -- a name with kingly roots. But his father was a Roman citizen, and he was also given the Latin name, Paul, or Paulus, which means "small". In the years when he identified as the Pharisee of Pharisees, Saul seemed like an appropriate name. But now his identity had changed -- he was now the Apostle to the Gentiles. The man who had wanted to be everything, now made himself nothing, just as his Lord and Savior had done. Saul had been transformed from "kingly" to "small". He was now and forevermore, the servant Paul. Let Jesus change your name.

He Believed

June 21

Read Acts 13:12; Galatians 3:5-9

When God opened the proconsul's eyes to see the works of the Lord, he was amazed at Paul's teaching, and he believed. "He believed!" -- two of the most beautiful words in Scripture. Paul was bold in his proclamation and it opened the way for the proconsul to believe. This is still our calling today -- to open the way for people to believe God. We are called to witness to God's glory in our worship, our giving, our testimony, our love, our prayers, and our service. When we live this way on a daily basis, a way is opened up for people to believe. Those with eyes to see, come to faith and see Jesus. We can partner with the Lord. Does your life's witness open the way for people to come to Jesus, or does it close the door in their faces? Strive to live in a way that blesses others and opens the way to God. Pray that you get to hear those two most beautiful words: "He (or she) believed."

Transformed to Preach

June 22

Read Acts 13:13-16; 1 Cor. 9:16-23

When Paul and Barnabas reached Pisidian Antioch, Paul got a request that every preacher loves to hear: "If you have a message, please speak." Saul the persecutor has become Paul the preacher. When Jesus takes hold of our life, He changes us so much that our old names don't fit anymore. Paul had experienced the transforming power of Jesus and was determined that the world should hear the gospel message. When he heard about Christ's call to "go and make disciples", he believed God and set out to intentionally evangelize as many as he could. And so Saul the murderer became Paul the missionary. Has Jesus transformed your life? He doesn't change us just so our life will be better… He changes us so that we can preach the gospel in some way to someone. We may never step behind a pulpit, but we are all called to share the gospel somewhere. Go!

Guide and Provider

June 23

Read Acts 13:16-22; Nehemiah 9:19-21

If we listen to God, He will guide us and provide for us, even in the deserts of life. God is real and wants a relationship with us. In the past He freed His people from bondage in Egypt, and led them through the desert to the Promised Land. He provided food and water for them every day. He provided light to guide them at night. In these last days, God has sent His Son as a light, and He calls people to follow Him. Those who have listened and believed have become His church. Christ not only sees them as followers, He calls them His Bride. If you are reading these words today as a believer, you are the Bride of Christ. He wants to be your guide and provider. Are you following Him? Are you faithful to him? If you are not a follower of Jesus, He is calling you. God is real and wants to have a relationship with you. Jesus will guide you and provide for you. He will light up your darkness. Answer His call.

The Savior Jesus

June 24

Read Acts 13:23-26; Luke 2:11; Matt. 4:17; Acts 2:38

God has sent us a Savior -- the Savior Jesus. God's grace-filled salvation message came to Earth in person as angels declared, "Today in the town of David, a Savior has been born to you." John preached that Christ was coming and that people should repent and be baptized. When Jesus came, He too called people to repentance. And after Christ's resurrection, Peter preached repentance unto salvation, calling people to turn to God and be baptized. The gospel message is consistent. God sent us a Savior. We are not worthy to untie the sandals of this Savior, yet He declared with His life that we are worth being saved. The gift of salvation has been sent to the children of Abraham and all God-fearing Gentiles. How can we not accept such a spectacular gift of love from our Creator? Believe, repent, and receive the Savior Jesus.

Blinded Eyes

June 25

Read Acts 13:27-29; 2 Cor. 4:3-6; John 1:10-13

Many people give the best years of their lives to an organization, receiving little or no recognition. Jesus understands. God came to Earth and walked among us, but we did not recognize Him. Instead of lifting Him up in worship, we lifted Him up on a cross. In our blindness, we condemned the Lord of Creation. Paul preaches that this was, and still is, an act of the will. People who are spiritually blind are blind by choice. They don't want to recognize Jesus as Lord. They don't want to change the way they live. They represent all of us, who at one time or another, have decided to go about our life without Jesus, without grace, and without salvation. In doing so, we join those in Jerusalem who condemned Jesus. By proxy, we nailed Christ to the cross in hopes that He would stop meddling in our lives. But He came back and is healing the spiritually blind on a daily basis. Choose to be healed.

A God Willed Resurrection

June 26

Read Acts 13:30-31; 1 Cor. 15:3-8

God raised Jesus from the dead. This was the heart of Paul's sermon because it is the heart of the Gospel. It is the beating heart of Christianity, and should be the main message of the church today. Jesus, who died on a cross for our sin, walked out of His tomb, and walked again with His people. Those who witnessed this told the story to anyone who would listen. They were so profoundly changed by the resurrection that they could not be silenced. This was the power that drove the early church. God had willed that a Savior be born and sacrificed for our sin. God willed a resurrection that changed everything. The church today can feed, heal, worship, pray, and fellowship, but without the resurrection we have no real message… no really good news… no hope for eternity. God willed the resurrection, and now His will is that we share the story. It's the least we can do.

Good News: Forgiveness of Sin

June 27

Read Acts 13:32-38; Matt. 26:27-28; Luke 24:46-47

Paul preached the good news -- the gospel of salvation. He was not confused or conflicted about the purpose of Christ's life, death, and resurrection. God fulfilled His promise when Jesus died on a cross and was raised to life. The death and resurrection of Jesus are directly tied to the forgiveness of sin -- sin which stands in the way of our relationship with the Creator both now and for eternity. His shed blood makes it possible for us to become a true child of God and receive God's blessing. We can be forgiven of our sins and reunited with our Father. Some today would de-emphasize Christ's shedding of blood for the forgiveness of sin. They say that a God of love would never plan for something as cruel as the cross. But God's love is precisely why Christ had to shed His blood -- it was poured out in love for the forgiveness of sins. Believe the good news. Accept His forgiveness.

Grace Comes Through Faith

June 28

Read Acts 13:39; Ephesians 2:4-9

"Through Him everyone who believes is justified." What a great truth of Scripture! What a great gift from God! Paul would later write in Ephesians, "It is by grace you have been saved, through your faith in Christ." No matter how hard they tried, God's people could not obtain righteousness or earn salvation by obeying God's Law. They could not be good enough or religious enough… neither can we! Instead, they had to decide whether or not to believe God and accept the gospel of truth… so will we. Salvation comes through Christ -- that's God's grace part. But we obtain it by believing God -- that's our faith part. We either choose to believe God and follow Jesus, or we choose to ignore the Gospel and continue going our own way. This is the proverbial fork in the road to our eternal destiny. What will it be for you -- faith or works? Grace or law? Saved or lost? The choice is yours.

Warning Against Unbelief

June 29

Read Acts 13:40-41; Malachi 4:1-6

Paul shares one more piece of the Gospel. It often gets left out today because it makes people uncomfortable, but without it the Gospel is incomplete. Believing the good news of Jesus is optional, but the consequences for unbelief are not. Paul quotes the prophet Habakkuk, who told God's people that a judgment was coming... because of their unfaithfulness they would be conquered by the Babylonians. Paul is saying, "Remember Babylon and choose wisely, for choices have consequences." There are two eternal destinations for all mankind -- one for those who put their faith in Christ, and another for those who do not. Every person reading this page will spend eternity in either Heaven or Hell based upon their choice to accept Christ and His sacrifice for sin, or to refuse God's grace and go their own way. Our faith makes a difference. The Gospel has not changed. Have you believed it?

Initial Success

June 30

Read Acts 13:42-44; Matthew 4:23-25

As Paul preached the good news of Jesus, there were those who wanted to hear more on the subject. Not everyone was hostile to the gospel, and so Paul and Barnabas were invited back to speak on the next Sabbath. When they returned the next week, the place was packed out. Just about everyone in the city was in attendance. The same kind of large crowds were attracted to Jesus early in His ministry. There are always some who are open to new things. There are always some who are seeking life in every city. Likewise, there will always be people who do not want to hear, and if we focus on these negative frowners and gripers we will only get frustrated. The gospel of God's grace is a grand truth that has the power to positively change lives. There will always be some who recognize that, and some who don't. Time is short. Preach to the living and to those seeking life.

Rising Stars Draw Fire

July 1

Read Acts 13:45; Acts 4:1-4; John 15:18-21

As Paul's star rose, his visibility drew negative attention. Rising up can bring glory to God, but it also makes one an excellent target. Satan cares little when you are ineffective in sharing Jesus, but if you start to draw a crowd, watch out. Paul's opposition arose from within the religious community. Religion is often possessive and jealous. It does not take kindly to competition or correction. Many a godly prophet preached their last sermon in front of a religious crowd, their reward for challenging the status quo coming in the form of physical or verbal stoning. Many churches today suffer from this mentality, as they claim exclusive rights to the truth. They compete more than they cooperate. Instead of praising God when someone gets saved, they curse men because they got saved somewhere else. Paul and Barnabas reaped the fruit of that spirit. Don't be a part of it today.

A Change of Direction

July 2

Read Acts 13:46-47; Isaiah 49:5-7

After Paul and Barnabas preached the gospel in the synagogue, they were verbally abused by the Jewish leaders. Being confident of their calling, they boldly answered those critics by quoting from the prophet Isaiah. If the Jews were going to turn a deaf ear toward Jesus, Paul and Barnabas would do something new -- they would take the salvation message directly to the Gentiles. Instead of changing the message, they changed directions. In marketing terms, they didn't change the product, they changed their marketing strategy. They would now preach Jesus to a completely different demographic. Great criticism can often be the stimulus for great change. Positive results can come out of negative feedback. Perhaps the constant criticism you have been receiving is God's way of prompting you to change direction and take the gospel somewhere new. Be open to change.

Appointed for Eternal Life

July 3

Read Acts 13:48-49; 1 Thess. 1:2-6; 1 Peter 1:1-2

When Paul and Barnabas took the gospel to the Gentiles, the results were immediate. The Gentiles responded enthusiastically, and those appointed for eternal life were saved. People who had never known God began to honor the word of the Lord, and the good news of Jesus began to spread throughout the region. Paul and Barnabas discovered that the gospel seemed to spread quickly among the Gentiles. Perhaps that is because religious people tend to think they need nothing, while those who are lost in the dark will always move toward a light when they see it. People who are hungry will eat food that others refuse. The gospel will catch fire among those who are dry and weary. The word of the Lord will spread when we share the gospel with those whose hearts have been prepared by God to receive it. This is what it means to be appointed for eternal life.

Shake The Dust Off Your Feet

July 4

Read Acts 13:50-51; Luke 9:1-6

Paul and Barnabas met with a high level of resistance in Pisidian Antioch, and decided to move on, taking the gospel down the road to Iconium. Before they left, they shook the dust off their feet -- a Middle Eastern sign of contempt. Jesus had instructed His disciples to do this if their message was rejected by a city or a group of people. It was a way of saying, "You had your chance to hear the truth, but you refused to listen. The consequences of your stubbornness are on your head, not ours." It is often difficult to decide whether to tough it out or move on, but this episode demonstrates that when it comes to sharing the gospel, there may indeed be a time to move on to greener pastures. Once someone has heard the gospel, whether or not they accept the truth, they have been evangelized. We are not responsible for the gospel's success. We are only responsible to share it with love.

Filled With Joy

July 5

Read Acts 13:52; Psalm 126:3-6

Paul and Barnabas and the disciples had plenty to complain about. Not everyone liked them. They had many enemies because of the gospel. They were run out of so many towns that they had automatic dust removers for their feet. They were disrespected, ejected, protested, arrested, and rejected. But they were filled with joy, because salvation and the Holy Spirit and joy go together. When people are being saved, it's hard to feel sorry for yourself. When God is moving and working through you it is difficult to be a whiner. Paul and the others genuinely believed that their life here on earth was about glorifying God, not about finding happiness. If and when we come to that same realization, we too can be filled with joy, and produce fruit for God's Kingdom in times of trials and testing. Difficult days will not defeat us when we see them as opportunities to glorify Christ.

Speaking Effectively For Jesus

July 6

Read Acts 14:1; 1 Cor. 16:8-9; Col. 4:3-6

Paul and Barnabas spoke so effectively in Iconium that great numbers of people believed. We are called to do the same. Speak effectively for the Lord. Never pass up the opportunity to witness about what Jesus has done in your life. You may face opposition from family, neighbors, our government, and perhaps even from religious people, but never assume this means your witness is ineffective. With words of grace and a life salted by Christ, press on and speak the truth in love. Become adept at sprinkling Jesus throughout your conversations. You don't have to be a preacher to do this. We should be seasoned with the love of Christ to the point that our everyday lives invite questions, and then we should be ready with an answer for people who ask why we are different. Make the most of every opportunity to share your story of God's mercy and love, and doors will open.

Truth Divides

July 7

Read Acts 14:2-4; 1 Thessalonians 2:2; John 7:40-43; Luke 12:49-53

Preaching and witnessing about Jesus causes division. The Name that brings peace also disturbs the peace. Jesus caused division. Truth always causes division. The church must never value holding the crowd, more than preaching the truth. We must not shade the truth, or compromise the gospel, in a quest to never be offensive. When the church values "unity" more than truth, and bodies more than souls, the gospel suffers. When we make "being together" more important than being saved, souls are at risk. The gospel brings salvation, but it also brings division. As witnesses for Jesus, we are not called to strive for unity, but to speak the truth in love. Some will believe and praise God -- others will mock the name of Jesus and curse us. Continue to speak the truth in love, and learn to live with the opposition and division it brings.

The High Cost of Ministry

July 8

Read Acts 14:5; Mark 11:18; John 5:18; Luke 10:1-3

Paul and Barnabas didn't just start arguments. They caused plots to be hatched -- plots to do them harm and kill them. Sometimes ministry comes at a very high cost. Jesus said it would be that way. He told the disciples that He was sending them out like lambs among wolves. This may come as a shock, but the Lord's greatest concern is not our personal safety. Instead, His chief concern is saving souls from hell. Jesus gave up His life to help accomplish that mission. What are you willing to give? When we do ministry, we may get roughed up. Sometimes the price may be even higher. But if we spend our lives avoiding danger, we will never excel at being a disciple. Paul's ministry came at a high cost, and so will yours. Will you pay the price? Millions of other disciples down through history have given their all. How much will you give?

Living to Preach Another Day

July 9

Read Acts 14:6-7; Matt. 9:36-38; Gal. 6:9

Paul and Barnabas became aware of a plot to kill them, and they fled. They did this more than once in their ministry, but they were never silenced by fear -- they just took the gospel message somewhere else. When we meet resistance it is not wrong to move on, but it is wrong to stop sharing the truth. Many Christians have been intimidated into becoming a "silent witness", which usually translates into "no witness at all". We go to church on Sunday, we go home, we go to work, and when we die people read our obituary and say, "Wow, I didn't know he was a Christian." There is nothing wrong with being prudent, but it is wrong to quit. Paul and Barnabas moved on, but they moved on for the purpose of living to preach another day. Do not become weary in doing what is right. The fields are ripe for the harvest. The work can be dangerous, but it is our calling. Don't quit!

Discerning Faith

July 10

Read Acts 14:8-10; Acts 3:1-7; Matthew 13:58; Luke 13:34

Because their time and resources were limited, Paul and Barnabas looked for those who had faith to believe. Two indicators of faith were a listening ear and good eye contact. When Paul looked into the eyes of the attentive crippled man, he saw faith. He saw willingness in the man's eyes. We cannot knock the doors down in people's lives -- faith must open the door from the inside before the Lord will enter. Jesus dealt with this early in His ministry, leaving Nazareth because of their lack of faith -- and near the end of His ministry, when He lamented Jerusalem's unwillingness to believe. Perhaps that is why He spent the majority of His time ministering in other places. Spend time with those who know they have a need -- those who want change in their life. It is difficult to bring healing to the faithless who think they are just fine.

Glory Thieves

July 11

Read Acts 14:11-18; Acts 12:21-23

At Lystra, Paul and Barnabas spoke God's healing over a man who had never walked, and the man jumped up and began walking. The crowd went wild and began to declare that "the gods" had come down to Earth. The glory that belongs to God alone was coming to Paul and Barnabas, but they would have none of it. We should be so wise. When your ministry becomes effective some may begin to praise you. Some may even begin to idolize you. It feels good to be treated like a rock star, but don't go there -- not even in your head. One of the worst things that can happen to Christians is for us to begin to feel like we deserve the accolades and the credit that come our way for being good people. We can begin to soak up the praise, but if we don't pass it on to the Lord, we become glory thieves, stealing what really belongs to God. Resist the temptation to become little gods.

He Got Up and Went Back

July 12

Read Acts 14:19-20; 2 Corinthians 1:8-11

As Paul preached in Lystra, religionists from Antioch and Iconium came and spoke against him. Convinced that Paul was a threat to their way of life, the crowd decided to stone Paul. When they finished, they dragged him out of the city and left him for dead. Being a disciple is not all fun and games. But the faithful gathered around him, and it would be foolish to think they weren't praying. Miraculously, Paul got up, and walked right back into the city where he had been attacked. He seemed to have no fear. Don't miss the importance of the community of faith praying here. We can do things we couldn't ordinarily do when we have the support and prayers of a community. That's why "lone ranger" Christianity is such a bad idea. But also don't miss the power of a life fully surrendered to God's sovereign will. Paul got up and went right back. That's courage! That's faith!

Continue to Evangelize

July 13

Read Acts 14:21; Acts 6:7; Acts 9:42

Wherever Paul and Barnabas went, they preached the Good News. They never stopped sharing the gospel. They never stopped witnessing and evangelizing. Many Christians today assume that most of those living and working around them have heard the gospel. That assumption is wrong. Reliable sources estimate that the un-churched population in the USA is near 150 million. The percentage of adults who do not regularly attend church continues to rise yearly. Statistics are even worse in many other nations around the globe. Believers, we have work to do. We must follow Jesus in a way that attracts people. Our witness must be consistent. We must find ways to lovingly share the gospel. Evangelism is more than an altar call. It is a life lived for Christ that shines like a light in the darkness. It is a loving and caring community. Never stop evangelizing.

Stronger Disciples

July 14

Read Acts 14:21-22; Matt. 28:18-20; Rev. 3:1-3

Paul and Barnabas knew it was important to disciple those that they had evangelized. They went back to the cities where they had preached the gospel, and taught them Christian basics. Jesus said, "Go into all the world and make disciples.", and so Paul and Barnabas discipled. Being a Christian is about more than just being saved -- it's about becoming more like Jesus every day, and growing progressively stronger in the faith. Any Christian who is not growing and strengthening their spiritual "legs" on a continual basis is not following the biblical pattern. Too many believers today think they have arrived. They think they've learned everything they need to know, but no one can ever reach that state on this side of heaven. Get back to learning in some way. Take a class. Read a book. Watch a good video series. Stretch, grow, and be strengthened. Become a genuine disciple.

The Gospel of Hardship

July 15

Read Acts 14:22; John 15:20, 16:33; 1 Peter 4:12

Paul and Barnabas experienced hardship as they preached the gospel. Their gospel was different from the one we often hear today -- it was a gospel of hardship. This gospel may not match up with our theology of prosperity and blessing, but it is documented in the pages of Scripture, and has been written in the blood of believers who have lived before us. This may sound like heresy in these days when the church is married to comfort and ease, but it would appear that hardship is sometimes God's will for His people. Jesus promised us that in this world we would have trouble: the apostle Peter said not to be surprised by painful trials we suffer, and Paul preaches that we must go through "many hardships to enter the kingdom of God". How many voices will it take before we get the message? We will need an enduring faith because the gospel is a gospel of hardship.

Appointing Leaders

July 16

Read Acts 14:23; Mark 3:13-15; Heb. 5:1-4

Paul and Barnabas knew that the churches they planted would need godly leaders. So they fasted and prayed for wisdom, asking God to show them who He wanted to lead His churches. When they discerned those leaders, they appointed them to be elders. Notice that this wasn't an election. It was an appointment to godly leadership by godly leaders. In doing this, Paul and Barnabas followed the ways of Jesus, who had also prayed and appointed disciples based on gifting and calling, rather than on popularity or education level. Too many times today, church leaders are chosen because of status, degrees, popularity, or how many books they have written. Paul and Barnabas looked more at whether or not a leader was gifted by God to teach the word, and whether or not that leader had a call to ministry. Churches would do well to follow that pattern today.

Maintaining Accountability

July 17

Read Acts 14:24-27; Luke 10:16-17; Mark 6:30-31

When Paul and Barnabas had finished their first missionary/church planting journey they returned to their home base in Antioch, and reported on what was accomplished. That's accountability. They gave glory to God for what He had done, and it wasn't for the purpose of raising funds. They were simply reporting -- being accountable to the brothers and sisters who had sent them out. Accountability is in short supply today. Be it individual Christians or large church bodies, we all covet "independence". One of the first questions asked by many church-shoppers is, "Are you part of a denomination?" Being "independent" is now seen as a great spiritual virtue. But this is not what we see in the New Testament church. Accountability was highly valued… by Jesus, and by Paul the apostle. In light of the biblical record, perhaps we need to rethink our penchant for valuing "independence".

Come Apart and Rest

July 18

Read Acts 14:28; Mark 6:31

After Paul and Barnabas reported on the churches they had planted, Scripture says they stayed in Antioch a long time. After an extended time in dangerous and high-pressure situations, they needed to rest and recharge, and that's what they did. They would go out again, for that was their calling -- but for a time they had no qualms about taking it easy in order to regain their strength. Even apostles need rest. Jesus taught this concept to his disciples and we would do well to follow suit. In Mark 6:31, Jesus led His disciples to a quiet place where they could get some rest. Some older translations have Jesus saying, "Come apart with me for a while." There is a Sabbath principle at work here, for even today, if we do not "come apart" for rest, we will eventually come apart. Constant work and stress with no relief, leads to breakdowns. Work hard for Jesus, but also take time to rest.

Sharp Dispute

July 19

Read Acts 15:1-2; Acts 15:5

Paul and Barnabas preached the gospel to the Gentiles, and many were saved. But then some Pharisees came from Jerusalem and told the new converts, "You must do more. If you want to really get right with God, you must obey all the Laws of Moses and be circumcised." Paul and Barnabas disputed this claim, and a heated argument ensued. The debate was so significant that a council meeting with the apostles and elders of the Church was organized in Jerusalem. Paul and Barnabas did not just go off and start a new group of their own. They knew that the Church belonged to Christ, not them. They preached accountability, and practiced accountability. Some of the greatest doctrines of the Church have evolved from great disputes. Disagreement is not a bad thing when it seeks truth, and leads to prayer and godly dialogue.

Blessing the Church

July 20

Read Acts 15:3-4; Gen. 12:1-3; Psa. 89:15-17

When Paul and Barnabas were sent to Jerusalem, they were sent as representatives of the church. They sought the council of others and went in the name of others. They did not act as lone wolves, but as shepherds of a flock. They preached their way to Jerusalem, stopping several times to tell the story of Gentile conversions. They had been blessed by the church, and they became a blessing to the church. Are you a blessing to your church? If you told the story of what God has done through you in the last year, would it make people glad? Would the church rejoice if you shared about who had come to the Lord this year through your ministry? All of us are either a blessing to the church or a drain on the church. We all start out needing something, but the goal is that we grow to the point of contributing something. Be a blessing today!

A God of Order

July 21

Read Acts 15:6-7, 12-13; 1 Cor. 14:29-33

Our God is a God of order. When the apostles and elders met in Jerusalem, it was an orderly meeting. When Paul rose to speak, everyone became silent. Many opinions were shared, with mutual respect and order. Each spoke in turn, the others listened, and they reasoned together. This discipline has been lost in our culture today. Orderly debate is a rare commodity. Listen to any news show or talk show where more than one person is involved and you will find that they operate by the rule of who can talk the loudest without taking a breath. Interruption and talking over others are standard fare. Chaos and disorder seem to rule the day. This is the way of the world, not God. Not everyone needs to hear your opinion whenever you feel like speaking. Tone it down. Wait your turn. Be polite. Listen more. Talk less. If we do this, the world will be a better place, and so will the church.

Star-Studded Cast

July 22

Read Acts 15:7, 12-13; Matthew 11:7-11

When that first great council meeting took place in Jerusalem, all the big names were there: Peter, Paul, Barnabas, James. They didn't likely know it, but they would become the heroes and superstars of the early church. Later generations would look up to them and imitate their faith and zeal. Children would be named after them. Yet these big names were just everyday ordinary people like us until they met an extraordinary Lord and Savior named Jesus. If you are a believer today, you have met the same Jesus that they met, and your life can become as extraordinary as theirs. The least in the kingdom of Heaven can become great. We will have to lay down our lives like they did. We will need to care about Jesus and His gospel more than we care about ourselves. But if we do, we can become part of a star-studded cast that changes the world. Who will be named after you?

Guided By Scripture

July 23

Read Acts 15:13-18; Rom. 10:11-17; 2 Tim. 3:16

At the Jerusalem Council, the early church established that Scripture, not tradition, should guide the church when they speak and act. After many had spoken, James stood and quoted the prophet Amos. It was clear to him that Scripture called for the Gentiles to be included in the church. The gospel was for them too. God had spoken! It was up to the church to find a way to obey the Lord. When Scripture guides our decisions and actions, we can walk that narrow road described by Jesus. When something else guides us, we will soon find ourselves in the ditch. When a church abandons the authority of Scripture, they soon devolve into just another social group or service club. Do not go there! The church must be anchored in, gathered around, and guided by the word of God, or it becomes like any other human organization. Jesus expects more of His Bride.

Agreeing With God

July 24

***Read Acts 15:28; John 14:16-17, 26;
2 Peter 1:19-21***

Jesus told His disciples that He would not leave them alone. He would send them a Counselor -- the Holy Spirit, who would guide them and empower them. Jesus kept His promise. Today, we who believe have this same Holy Spirit to direct us. He helps us interpret and understand Scripture. He lights our path as we traverse the narrow way. Christ calls us to live out His teaching and walk in harmony with the Holy Spirit. When we live our lives in cooperation with the Counselor, we cease making decisions all on our own and solely for our personal benefit. This was the strength of the early church. In so many different areas of life, they could say with integrity, "It seemed good to the Holy Spirit and to us." When we can also say with integrity that we are in agreement with the Holy Spirit, we will make godly decisions that glorify the Lord.

Leadership Decision

July 25

Read Acts 15:13, 19; Heb. 13:7, 17; 1 Cor. 11:1

The Council of Jerusalem ended with a leadership decision. James, the leader of the church in Jerusalem, spoke up and said, "I've heard all the arguments. We've prayed and listened to God for a time. And now, here's my decision. This is the direction we are going to go." As far as we know, there was no vote taken that day. They took time to build consensus, but there is no record of any official vote. The church, contrary to what many believe, has never been a democracy. James had been called to lead, and he acted like a leader. He had been entrusted by God to lead the church in Jerusalem, and on this day he spoke with the authority that God had bestowed upon him. This decision by James set a precedent for the early church -- one that has not changed. Salvation comes by grace through faith, not through obedience to the Law. It was a good decision

Equal Opportunity Savior

July 26

Read Acts 15:7; Romans 10:1-13

Jesus is an equal opportunity Savior. Peter learned this when he preached to the Gentiles and they received the Holy Spirit -- the same Holy Spirit that the Jewish disciples had received. Peter concluded that God makes no distinction between Jew and Gentile when it comes to salvation. Paul the apostle came to this same conclusion. He advocated for Gentiles to be included as full members of the Church, without requiring circumcision. Salvation comes by grace through faith to all who believe. Jesus came to save every lost person. He died for the sins of the whole world. Peter said that God "made no distinction". Paul said "there is no difference". Everyone who calls on the name of the Lord can be saved. Anyone whose heart had been purified by faith was welcome in the body of Christ. This was the "big tent" policy of the early church. Is this your church's policy?

Boundaries Not Barriers

July 27

Read Acts 15:19, 28-29; Eph. 2:11-22

James made a grace-filled statement at the end of the Council of Jerusalem. Basically he said, "Let's keep it simple, and not make it difficult for people to turn to Christ. It shouldn't be hard to get into the church. Let's do away with the legalistic burdens. The church should be about inviting people in, not about keeping people out. The church will have some boundaries, but it shouldn't be about building barriers." James called for a few basic requirements regarding food sacrificed to idols and sexual immorality, but other than that, the church was open to all sinners saved by God's amazing grace. Christ's church should be accessible to all those seeking and celebrating salvation. Some basic boundaries are necessary, but the church should not be in the business of creating barriers. We are called to labor at bringing them in… not work to keep them out.

Grace and Faith

July 28

Read Acts 15:9-11; Ephesians 2:4-9

The early church made a strategic decision at the Council of Jerusalem. They came to a fork in the road and they took the Jesus way. No longer would they teach that salvation comes through obedience to the Law of Moses. Many were still Jewish by birth, but they had become something else -- they had become disciples of Jesus, the incarnation of God who came to die for the sins of the world. The church declared that salvation comes by grace through faith to all who believe, Jew and Gentile alike. God had purified the hearts of both Jews and Gentiles because of His grace and their faith. This is still the good news. This is what makes the church distinctly Christian. This is what makes it possible for all to be saved. It is by God's grace, but it takes a decision of faith. Have you made that decision? Will you put your faith in Christ? From now until the day you die, you will not get a better offer.

Center of Glorious Conflict

July 29

Read Acts 15:30-35; Acts 11:19-30; Gal. 2:11-16

Antioch was both a command center and an oasis for Paul and Barnabas. The church there was a hybrid, made up of both Jews and Gentiles. This was a great strength, but also led to Antioch being at the center of some glorious conflict in church history. They were a generous church, sending monetary aid to Judea in time of great need, and financing Paul and Barnabas on their missionary journeys. Antioch was central in the dispute that led to the Council of Jerusalem, where the church established the gospel's freedom from Jewish law. Antioch was also the site of a great showdown between Peter and Paul over justification through faith alone, rather than by observing the law. Antioch, where believers were first called Christians, was on the cutting edge of church growth. This one local church changed the course of history. Will history say that about your church?

More Than Evangelists

July 30

Read Acts 15:36; Matt. 28:18-20; Luke 14:33

Paul and Barnabas were heroes in the church. They had evangelized many people, and started churches all around the Mediterranean. But God called them to be more than evangelists. The Lord had called them to make disciples and grow churches. They could have stayed in Antioch, kicked back, and written "how-to" books, but instead, they went back out to check on the churches they had planted and disciple them. They took Christ's admonition to "make disciples" seriously. They saw these new believers as more than just a notch in their belts. They gave up everything to go back and disciple those they had led to the Lord. We must never stop evangelizing, but we must also make disciples. Saving souls and teaching believers to obey the Lord are like two sides of the same coin. We won't get our "money's worth" out of Christianity unless we see that both get done.

The First Church Split

July 31

Read Acts 15:37-41; Genesis 13:5-12

When two people "part company" it is not always pretty. It can be even uglier when it happens in the church. But it happens, and it happens to the best… even Paul and Barnabas. They had what Luke describes as a "sharp disagreement". It wasn't about a deep theological issue -- it was a personnel issue. Barnabas, the church board chair, wanted Mark on the staff, and Paul, the preacher, didn't. It was a typical power struggle. Harsh words were spoken, they parted ways, and we witness the first church split recorded in Scripture. Even though this was not likely God's plan, the Spirit of God went with both of them, and the evangelism/discipleship capability of the church was effectively doubled as they opened two separate mission fields. We don't have to be perfect for God to use us. We should strive to be as good as we can be, but God will be glorified in spite of our personal successes and failures.

A Book of Truth

August 1

Read Acts 15:37-40; Colossians 4:10

The argument between Paul and Barnabas over John Mark was so serious that they parted company. How did two godly apostles reach this point? We find a clue in Paul's letter to the Colossians -- John Mark was a cousin to Barnabas. Mark and Barnabas were family, and we all know the old adage about blood being thicker than water. Paul may have been stubborn, but Barnabas was working with a strong bias, and because of that they ended up at a fork in the road. This dynamic duo had what we call today an internal dispute, and it split the team apart. This was certainly not one of the church's finest moments, but it is a good reason to trust the Bible. Scripture shows God's people for who they are, warts and all. It doesn't try to do a PR job for the church. God just lays it out there -- the good, the bad, and the ugly. We can trust the word of God to tell us the truth.

Double Edged Ministry

August 2

Read Acts 15:39b-41; Isa. 61:7; Heb. 4:12

God can redeem anything for His glory -- even sharp disagreements that would appear to weaken the church. When Barnabas and Paul went their separate ways, Barnabas took Mark and went to Cyprus where the work of the Lord expanded, and Paul picked up a young disciple named Silas and went through Syria and Cilicia, strengthening the church and winning many to Jesus. What looked like a victory for Satan instead became double trouble. One team had become two teams. Gospel proclamation had doubled overnight. Paul and Barnabas had become a two-edged sword. The gospel was now on the offensive on two fronts. It may not have been in God's original plan for Paul and Barnabas to split up, but God used it to His advantage. God knows how to win with any set of circumstances. God can redeem anything for His glory, even our human failings.

Time Heals

August 3

Read Acts 15:37-39; Philemon 1:23-24; 2 Tim. 4:11

The passage of time can soften anger and heal wounds. Things that once seemed so important can seem trivial years later. This happened with Mark and Paul. Mark, who had caused a split between Paul and Barnabas, became someone Paul wanted by his side -- a trusted ally in the work of the gospel. In Paul's letter to Philemon, Mark is listed as one of Paul's "fellow workers". And later, when Paul wrote to his young disciple Timothy, he mentioned Mark as being "helpful" to his ministry. We don't know what happened, but somehow Paul and Mark had reconciled. Perhaps Paul realized that the grace he preached so vehemently needed to be applied to Mark. Maybe Mark matured, grew stronger, and proved himself to be reliable. The bottom line is that people can change. We can change. Things do not stay the same forever here on Earth. Thank God for that! Time heals.

Failure is Never Final

August 4

Read Acts 15:39b-41; 1 Peter 5:12-13

There is no doubt that Mark failed in his younger days. The biblical record is clear. But he wasn't content to be known as a failure. Mark kept working at the faith. Over time he became a "go-to guy" in the church, and ended up writing one of the four gospels that we read today. This young man who bailed out early in his spiritual walk, ended up on the "A-List" of major apostles. Mark not only ended up on Paul's list of friends, he became like a son to Peter. Perhaps Peter identified with Mark, as he also had a notorious failure in his past. If anyone understood overcoming failure, it would have been Peter. Failure is never final! It wasn't for Peter. It wasn't for Mark. And it need not be for you. The only way that failure is ever final is if you quit. Don't do that! Don't miss what God has for you down the road. If you have stumbled, get back up. Run again. Finish the race. Don't give up!

Disciple Maker

August 5

Read Acts 16:1-3; Matthew 28:19-20

Paul didn't just take his salvation and run. He didn't just "pray the prayer" and continue living like he did before. His salvation was more than just fire insurance. Paul became a disciple, and then became a disciple-maker. He became a follower, and then produced more followers. He obeyed the Great Commission, which is a command of Christ. Paul was a leader, and he produced leaders. Silas and Timothy learned to follow Jesus by following Paul. He did not invite Silas and Timothy to become students -- he called them to become disciples. The two are not necessarily the same thing. A disciple is more than just a learner -- he is a follower, an adherent, and an imitator. The goal of a disciple is not just to know what the teacher knows, but to live like the teacher lives. We should be good disciples, but in time, we should become disciple- makers. Are you a disciple-maker?

Teacher and Leader

August 6

Read Acts 16:4; Hebrews 5:11-6:3

Paul was both a teacher and a leader. He was willing to get out in front and say, "Here's the way we should go." He went from town to town delivering decisions, and declaring, "Thus saith the Lord." That can be uncomfortable at times, and it can make you a target, but it was his calling. We are all called to teach and lead someone in some way. Christians are called to do more than just accumulate knowledge and faith -- God calls us to pass it on. We should all be teaching someone. We may never lead big groups or preach to large crowds, but we can all lead someone. Look for opportunities to teach and lead. God has enough reluctant believers who want to just kick back and enjoy the ride. What the Lord needs are Christians who will do more than follow and learn. Jesus needs disciples who will lead and teach. He needs disciples who will disciple.

Growing Churches

August 7

Read Acts 16:5; Acts 2:46-47; Acts 6:7

Sometimes ministries get out of focus and become more about numbers than about people. But the opposite is also true. There are far too many churches today that are apathetic about numbers. God wants us to grow. It's the natural result of prayer, proclamation, and discipleship. It's a part of organic Christianity. Scattered throughout the book of Acts are verses about continual growth in number. God wants His kingdom to grow, and when His kingdom grows, His church grows. There are some mechanics involved in this, but if every Christian in your city was praying, witnessing, loving, evangelizing, and discipling, churches in your city would be growing. Very few believers set these kinds of spiritual goals for themselves. Other things dominate our thinking and consume our time. Grow the kingdom. It's one of the signs of life. Things must grow, or they die.

A Stop and Go God

August 8

Read Acts 16:6-12; Jonah 1:1-3

God kept Paul from going to Asia and Bithynia, but called him to Macedonia. We don't know how God communicated the message in each case, but one thing is clear: Paul heard God because he was listening. Three times God spoke to Paul -- three times Paul heard and obeyed. Christians, we must learn to hear God. We cannot live with godly wisdom until we learn to hear the Lord. This is not natural for us. It is a discipline. We must practice at it. Sometimes God stops us from going where we think we ought to go. When this happens, we must stay put and wait for direction. Sometimes the Lord sends us to where we never thought we would go. When that happens, we must go. If we fail to listen and obey on either side of this equation, like Jonah, we are doomed to end up on roads we were never supposed to take, and in places we were never intended to be. Listen and obey.

God Knows Where

August 9

Read Acts 16:6-9; Jonah 3:1-5

Scripture often tells of God calling someone to go somewhere to do a task for Him. Then that person either goes or refuses to go. But today, Paul is ready, willing, and able to go, and God stops him from going. The Holy Spirit kept Paul from preaching in the province of Asia, and then the Spirit of Jesus stopped Him from entering Bithynia. God prevented Paul from going places where there were certainly lost people. God made one place a priority over others. Why? This may come as a surprise to some, but God knows more than we do. He knows where hearts are open to truth. He knows where He wants us to be and who is open to the gospel. God knew Macedonia was fertile soil, just like God knew the Ninevites were ready to repent in Jonah's day. All God needed was obedient preachers. God knows a place and a people where your witness is needed. Listen for Him and go there.

A Gospel for the Wealthy

August 10

Read Acts 16:11-15; Luke 19:1-10; James 2:19

Paul's mission team traveled to Philippi in Macedonia, where they met a woman named Lydia who was a "dealer in purple cloth". Purple cloth was worn by royalty, high government officials, and the very wealthy. Lydia didn't just run a small retail store, she was a wholesaler. This means that a wealthy business woman was Paul's first convert in Macedonia. The gospel of Jesus Christ is not just for the poor. Jesus also died for those who are rich. Lydia believed in God, but was not a Christian. She was "a worshipper of God", but still needed to hear the gospel, believe, and be born again. Many people today say they believe in God, and think that this makes them a "Christian". But believing in God, even being a worshipper of God, is not enough. We must be saved by grace, through faith, and surrender our lives to Jesus Christ. Rich or poor alike must come to know and follow the Son.

A Gospel for Those in Bondage

August 11

Read Acts 16:16-18; Luke 4:31-37

Jesus came to set the captives free. He died for the poor as well as for the wealthy. He saves the weak and the powerful. Paul's first convert in Philippi was a wealthy businesswoman… his second was a spirit-possessed slave girl. That's diversity! The slave girl would have been the polar opposite of Lydia. She was part of a lower class of people who were seen as human chattel by those who owned them. To her owners, she was a possession, not a person -- but Paul saw a woman possessed by more than just men. She had an evil spirit that told fortunes, and her owners used her to make money. She was a spiritual prostitute. But then she heard the name of Jesus as Paul spoke freedom into her life, silencing the voices of darkness that came from her mouth. The Most High God set her free. Christ wants to do that for you. Are you free? In the name of Jesus, be free!

The Greatest Question

August 12

Read Acts 16:23-34; 1 Thess. 5:16-18

After Paul and Silas freed the slave girl from an evil spirit, they were arrested, beaten, and thrown into jail. Later, they were heard singing praises to God. Light can shine, even from dark prison cells. One of those listening was the Roman jailer. Rome had strict rules for jailers. If anyone escaped during your watch, you were executed. So when an earthquake came, and the cell doors sprang open, the jailer assumed everyone had escaped. He was about to kill himself when Paul assured him that no one was missing. Realizing it was a miracle, the jailer fell on his knees and asked the greatest question one can ever ask: "What must I do to be saved?" Paul and Silas shared the gospel with him, and he and his household became believers. We can learn from this. When we praise God in difficult times, He can make great things happen. And if you haven't asked the greatest question… ask it!

The Great Melting Pot

August 13

Read Acts 16:14; Acts 16:16; Acts 16:29-34

The early church was a melting pot. In Philippi, God put an upper class wealthy female business executive together with a formerly demon-possessed slave girl and a sturdy middle class Roman jailer. People who would never have associated before Jesus came together around the cross of Christ. Lives that had nothing in common except salvation had their hearts melted together by the fire of the Holy Spirit. What a grand idea! Christ still wants His church to be a melting pot. But today, instead of asking God, "Where could I be used the most for the glory of your Kingdom?" we go church shopping for the group that is most like us. We look for a church that will serve our needs, rather than a church where we can serve the needs of others. We end up in churches with a common income level, a common skin color, and a common family status. And we're all poorer for it.

An Earthly Reward for Faithfulness

August 14

Read Acts 16:19-24; Acts 7:54-60

This may come as a surprise, but the earthly reward for faithfulness may be hate and persecution. Sharing Christ may get you a kick in the stomach, rather than a pat on the back. Paul and Silas saw a woman who needed to be set free from a dark spirit, and for their act of mercy, they were beaten and arrested. This still happens in many parts of the world today where Christians refuse to compromise their faith and witness. Not everyone will be happy that Jesus set you free -- it threatens the spirit of darkness in their lives. People you partied with will often view your conversion with disdain, rather than as a touching story of a soul set free. Tell your story anyway. Sing God's praises even in the dark places of life. Love people. Tell them why you've changed when they notice you are different. Don't let the hate discourage or silence you.

Praise Quotient

August 15

Read Acts 16:25; Heb. 13:15; Psa. 34:1-4

Acts 16:25 is an astounding verse. After Paul and Silas were beaten and confined to a jail cell, they had a worship service. There was no bitter complaining about the injustice -- just praise to God in such a public way that others around them could hear it. They responded to a life that is unfair, by giving glory to God. They didn't question God's goodness -- they praised God's greatness. They thanked God for a demon cast out, for souls saved, and for a new church plant. They had surrendered their lives to the glory of God. How are you doing at this? What was your praise quotient last week? Our praise quotient is the number of times we praise God, divided by the number of times we complain about God -- the bigger the number the better. Raise your quotient. Praise more and complain less. You'll be noticed by those around you, and some will be drawn to the One you praise.

<u>A</u>dmit, <u>C</u>ommit, <u>T</u>ransmit, <u>S</u>ubmit

August 16

Read Acts 16:25, 29-34; Matthew 7:20-21

The conversion of the Roman jailer provides a template for evangelism. First we must ADMIT. The jailer admitted his need for a Savior. The second step is to COMMIT. The jailer was called to "believe in the Lord Jesus." This was a commitment to follow Christ as Lord -- to be His disciple. The third step is to SUBMIT. The jailer was baptized in obedience to Christ and began to minister to Paul and Silas. Conversion brings life change as we submit to Christ's call to serve. "By their fruit you will know them." The fourth component in evangelism is to TRANSMIT. Paul and Silas "spoke the word of the Lord to him." They had first transmitted the gospel with the fruit of joy displayed in jail, then later, with words of truth. They reflected the Way and the Truth well, and thus were believed when they spoke the truth about the way. Admit, Commit, Submit, Transmit -- one template for evangelism.

So That Some Might Be Saved

August 17

***Read Acts 16:14; 16:16-18; 16:29-33;
Matthew 7:13-14; 1 Corinthians 9:19-23***

When Paul and Silas went down to the river and met Lydia, she responded to the gospel. Others were there and heard, but we have no record that anyone else was saved. When Paul and Silas delivered the slave girl from demonic spirits, there were many witnesses. But not everyone who saw the miracle was converted. When Paul and Silas led the Roman jailer to Christ, there were others who heard the truth. But not everyone at the jail became a believer. Even though God so loves the world and Jesus died for the sins of the world, not everyone in the world will be saved. Jesus said the road is narrow and only a few will find it. Paul recognized that even with the best of preaching, "by all possible means", only "some" would be saved. Be faithful in sharing the gospel, but do not be discouraged when only a few respond.

The Blessing of Persecution

August 18

Read Acts 16:40: Matt. 5:10-12; John 15:18-21

When Paul and Silas got out of prison, they went back to Lydia's house for some renewal and rest. They met with the new believers there, and then headed out again to share the gospel in another place. Paul and Silas traveled a road that few are willing to travel. Instead of being thwarted by persecution, they were motivated. Persecution does a strange thing to a committed believer. Instead of silencing us, it often ends up strengthening us. If we are active enough to receive persecution, and we endure it with grace, it often gives us a greater platform from which to share the gospel. If you are undergoing persecution in some form, remember this story. Endure it with grace. Live with hope in your heart. Stand strong and humbly praise God. If you do that, your Jesus star will rise and be seen by more people than ever, and God's kingdom will grow because of your faithfulness.

Reason and Faith

August 19

Read Acts 17:1-3; Acts 10:39-43; Matt. 16:13-18

Even though Paul was sent to evangelize the Gentiles, he never gave up on his fellow Jews, and often went to the synagogues to preach. At Thessalonica he taught three weeks in a row, reasoning with them "from the Scriptures", or what we call the Old Testament. Using the Old Testament, Paul proved and explained that Christ had to suffer and rise from the dead. Paul echoed Peter, who taught that all the prophets testified about Jesus and that through His name, all who believe in Him will receive forgiveness of sins. Some say reason and faith do not mix, but Paul would disagree. He often reasoned from the Scriptures to bring people to faith. He wanted everyone to believe that Jesus is the Christ, for through faith comes forgiveness of sins and eternal salvation. That was true in Paul's day, and it is still true today. Put your faith in Jesus Christ. It's the reasonable thing to do.

Win Some, Lose Some

August 20

Read Acts 17:4-5; 1 Cor. 9:16; Luke 4:42-44

After being beaten and jailed in Philippi, Paul and Silas moved down the road to Thessalonica. They weren't looking for a friendlier place, or a better deal -- they were looking for more people who needed the Lord. When they preached in Thessalonica, some received the truth and joined with them. Others chose to oppose the message of God and stirred up trouble. It has always been that way, and it will always be that way. We win some, and lose some. Some will respond to the gospel -- others will reject it. We don't get to choose who does which. God's Spirit opens the ears and eyes of some, but others will go to their graves deaf and blind to the grace of God. Nothing you or anyone else can say will soften their hard hearts. But still, we keep saying it. We cast out God's seed and where it falls and sprouts is God's business. We aren't called to be successful -- we are called to be faithful.

Guilt By Association

August 21

Read Acts 17:6-9; Luke 21:12-19

After Jason invited Paul and Silas to come to his house, he discovered that just being around committed Christians can cost you. A hostile mob invaded his home and when they didn't find Paul or Silas, they dragged Jason and some "other brothers" to the authorities. Jason got in trouble for just hanging around with committed Christians. Today, some people will wrinkle up their noses when they find out that you go to church. You don't even have to talk about Jesus, all you have to do is associate with people of faith, and you become a target for ridicule. Why is that? It's because Satan knows that he cannot allow even one ray of light to invade his darkness. He fears the name of Jesus, and does not want people to even get near it. So he tries to keep people away from committed Christians. Our goal is to be committed enough that the devil must try to keep people away from us!

Blessed Are The Troublemakers

August 22

Read Acts 17:6; Acts 24:5-6; Heb. 10:32-35

The mob that rioted in Thessalonica resembled the mobs of today, blaming someone else for their bad behavior. They pointed to Paul and Silas, and accused them of making trouble all over the world. That's quite a claim! Would anyone say that about you? Is your faith so active and far-reaching that you would be accused of making trouble all over the world? Would it surprise you to know that God will bless the right kind of troublemaker? Paul and Silas did nothing wrong. They simply preached the truth and challenged the status quo religion. They shared the love of God, delivered people from demons, and spoke of Christ's death and resurrection wherever they went. Because of this, they were accused of causing trouble all over the world. If that's the kind of trouble you cause in this world, Jesus would likely say, "Blessed are the troublemakers."

Like A Broken Record

August 23

Read Acts 17:10; 2 Corinthians 11:23-28

Paul's life played out like a broken record. For those too young to remember, when an old phonograph record got a deep scratch or a crack in it, it would often skip, playing the same phrase over and over again. Today's verses repeat the now familiar story of Paul being run out of town. Over and over again, this was his earthly reward for preaching the truth. The true gospel is offensive. It changes people, and many don't want to see that happen. More than once, Paul got beaten up and close to killed. Again and again, he had to flee for his life. This is because Paul was a persistent prophet. The first thing Paul and Silas did when they reached Berea was to go to the synagogue. They didn't go there for a handout -- they went there to preach the gospel of Jesus Christ as Lord and Savior. Thank God for persistent prophets whose lives play out like broken records.

Eager Beaver Bereans

August 24

Read Acts 17:11; Matt. 13:23; Rom. 15:4

Luke describes the Bereans as being of "noble character". What does that look like? Scripture says the Bereans "received the message with great eagerness." They eagerly received the gospel that Jesus died for their sin and rose again. They also likely shared that message with enthusiasm. They became gossips for the gospel. Can you imagine a church where all of the gossip pertained to the good news of Jesus, rather than the perceived failings of others? The church's reputation could change almost overnight. We could become like the Bereans and be thought of as "noble in character". But it all starts with us receiving the message with eagerness. Believe the good news. Receive Jesus Christ as Lord and Savior. If you're tired of the character you've become, and would like to become a person of noble character, this is where you start. It's where the Bereans started.

Daily Examination

August 25

Read Acts 17:11; Luke 11:3; 1 Thess. 2:13

The Bereans didn't read Scripture because they thought it would impress God, or make them look more holy. They examined the Scriptures daily to hear from God. They read seeking truth. They read God's word every day to verify that what Paul preached was the truth. They spent considerable time diligently studying the word of God. They are a model for us. Many Christians today are long on feelings, but short on knowledge of Scripture. The majority have never read the Bible through. Examining the Scriptures daily is a foreign concept. They may attend church regularly, but seldom open their Bibles outside the church building. In so doing, they miss out on God's daily bread, and on one of the Lord's greatest tools for producing noble character. Don't join them in their negligence. Be different! Get into the word. Be among those who examine the Scriptures on a daily basis.

Daily Bible Study

August 26

Read Acts 17:11; 1 Cor. 2:12, 14; James 1:22

Daily Bible study is a vital tool for the disciple of Jesus. Here are some hints on how to become more like the Bereans. First, find a translation you understand. There are many, and most of them are good. Second, find a reading plan and stick to it. God is a God of order. It makes sense to use an orderly plan for reading the Bible. Third, ask the Holy Spirit to speak through the Scriptures. We need God's help to understand. Ask God to open your ears and your heart so you can hear what He is saying. Fourth, as you read, ask two questions: what does it say, and what does it say to me? In other words, what did it mean then, and what does it mean to me today? Fifth, be faithful in personal application and obedience. Once we know what God is saying to us, we need to do what the Lord says. Without this last step, the Bible is just words on paper. God wrote it to be far more than that.

History Repeats Itself

August 27

Read Acts 17:12; Acts 13:49-50;
Acts 14:1-2; 1 Thessalonians 2:1-4

Wherever Paul preached, some believed and gave their lives to Christ. But there were always those who criticized and threatened. Paul faced opposition in every town, in every conceivable form – and often it became physical. You could always count on pushback. It was inevitable, as history repeated itself over and over again. But Paul would not quit. He was like a pit bull for the gospel. He would not let go. He would not stop talking about Jesus. He would not quit, because he had been called and because everywhere he went, someone got saved. That made it worth the risk and the pain. Is that your philosophy of ministry as a Christian? Will you push through the pushback for the sake of a soul saved? Like Paul, this is our calling. Accept the inevitable opposition and keep speaking the truth in love. Souls are at stake.

Idolatry Run Amok

August 28

Read Acts 17:16; 1 John 5:21; Exodus 20:2-5

Paul went to Athens, a very cosmopolitan and sophisticated city, full of highly educated and intelligent people. But Paul saw something that disturbed his spirit. This modern metropolis was filled with idols. The many shrines and altars there betrayed a polytheistic culture. These people were very religious. They had a shrine for every god except the true God. Paul was highly educated and certainly knew of Athens before he was saved. But now he came with new eyes… eyes opened by the Holy Spirit, and what he saw was idolatry run amok. And if our eyes are open, we can see the same thing today. We live in a polytheistic culture where individual choice reigns supreme. Our idols may not look the same as those in Athens, but they are numerous and powerful, and we bow down to them and worship them in various ways. Ask God to give you eyes to see the idols in your life.

Reasonably Opposing Idolatry

August 29

Read Acts 17:17; Acts 17:1-4; Isaiah 1:18-21

When Paul saw the rampant idolatry in Athens, he didn't just wring his hands, or complain to his Bible study group about how the world was going to hell in a hand basket. Armed with truth, he initiated a battle with them on two fronts. He reasoned with them in the synagogue (for us, that is the church), and he reasoned with them in the marketplace (for us, that is where we work and shop). He didn't rant, rave, and shout about people burning in hell. He wasn't hostile or condemning. Scripture says he reasoned with them. He told them of a God who could be known... a God who created all things... a God who could not be captured in an idol made of gold, stone, or wood. He spoke about judgment, repentance, and a man who rose from the dead. He had their attention. Paul shows us that we can reasonably oppose idolatry and that when we do, the hearts of some will be changed.

Babble On Believers

August 30

Read Acts 17:18; 1 Cor. 1:20-25; Col. 2:8

Paul proved that reasoning can work in evangelism, but no method is fool proof where man has both free will and pride. Some believed -- others debated Paul. When we share Jesus and His resurrection, we can expect opposition. In Athens, it was philosophers. Genuine and wannabe philosophers of today will usually attack us in one of two ways. First, there is the "put down". They called Paul a "babbler". Today it may be "bible thumper", "narrow minded", "holy roller", or a dozen other slanderous titles designed to make you feel stupid, out of touch, or ashamed. Second, the supposed philosopher will try to convince you that you are advocating foreign gods. They'll say stuff like, "I believe in God, but you've gone too far with this Jesus in your heart stuff. Don't get carried away with that wacko foreign thinking." Christian, do not listen to the philosophers of this age. Babble on!

The Best Idea

August 31

***Read Acts 17:19-21; 1 Timothy 6:20;
Mark 12:28-30; Romans 10:8-10***

Paul was brought before the Areopagus, a group
who spent all their time listening to and talking
about the latest ideas. They thought Paul's ideas
were strange and wanted to hear more. They
were trying to intellectualize the faith. Many
today try to do the same thing. As long as Jesus
remains just in the mind, and never moves into
the heart and soul, we can keep Him at a safe
distance. As long as Jesus is just a good idea,
He does not threaten our lifestyle and we don't
have to change. Other ideas and philosophies
are just as valid for managing our lives. Thus we
hear people say, "Jesus is fine if He works for
you -- just don't push your religion on me. I have
my own ideas about God -- my own personal
religion. Believe whatever you want." But Jesus
didn't come to be just a good idea. Jesus came
as God's best idea! Believe in your heart.

Covering Our Bases

September 1

Read Acts 17:22-23; John 14:6; Deut. 4:23-24

In the minds of the highly educated philosophers of Athens, it was wise to embrace every idea and every god. They celebrated the diversity of their culture and built altars to all the gods. Everybody's god was seen as equally valuable. The Athenians were so concerned about being inclusive that they even had an altar to the "UKNOWN GOD". They didn't want to risk leaving anyone out. This is called pluralism and it is still popular among the sophisticated and enlightened of our day. The inclusiveness of the Athenians would have been lauded by our contemporary culture. But Paul knew it was wrong. His Judaism told him that there was but one God, and his newfound faith in Christ had convinced him that there is but one Messiah and one way to salvation. His wisdom holds true today. There is but one covering for all of the bases. His name is Jesus. Let Him cover you.

Knowing the Unknown God

September 2

Read Acts 17:23b-26; Philippians 3:10-11

At the beginning of his presentation to the Areopagus, Paul told the highly educated Greek philosophers, "I know something you don't know. I know who the Unknown God is. In fact, I know the Unknown God personally. I have met the Unknown God." Paul then began to make known to them this Unknown God. He started with the truth of Genesis, telling them of the Creator God who gives life and breath to all things. This God is Spirit and does not live in manmade temples, nor does He live in idols made by human hands. From one man, this God made all nations. This God determines the length of our lives and where we live out those lives. This God is the sovereign Lord of all things. Paul went on later to proclaim that this God is the risen Christ. This is our calling, Christians. Our God, who is unknown to many, wants to be known, and we are called to make Him known. Share the truth.

Perhaps

September 3

Read Acts 17:27-28; Matthew 19:11; Luke 13:23-24; Romans 11:13-14

When we speak of Jesus in the way Paul did, God uses our words to win some. When we speak the truth in love, the Unknown God can become the known God. Some will realize that we "live and move and have our being" in Christ. Some will seek the Lord, and "perhaps reach out and find Him". He is near… but don't miss the word "perhaps". Not all will accept God's offer of grace. Even Jesus did not win everyone when He was here. He was the perfect Son of God, and yet many did not believe. All humanity has a free will. Every individual can choose to accept or reject Christ, and there will always be those who will refuse to believe. But we must not focus on the refusals. We must continue to be faithful in praying for the lost, reasoning with them, and lifting up our risen Lord Jesus. Our hope is that "perhaps" some will be saved.

Homemade Idolatry

September 4

***Read Acts 17:29; Isaiah 2:7-9;
Jeremiah 10:3-6; Jonah 2:8-9***

Idolatry is nothing new. Mankind has been drawn toward idols since Adam and Eve first sinned in the Garden. Whenever we place anything ahead of the interests of God, we have drifted into idolatry. Moses, Isaiah, Jeremiah, and many other prophets confronted it in their day, and when Paul got to Athens, he dealt with it there. Believers must continue to confront the idolatry in our world with God's truth, and the place we should start is in our own lives. What are the idols that demand your time, attention, and money? What steals your affection and allegiance? What is it that holds you back from serving Jesus fully? Idols don't have to be made of wood, stone, or gold -- they can be thoughts or activities that distance us from Jesus. Destroy them! Abandon them! Remove them from your homes and your lives. Worship the Living God!

Ignorance Is No Excuse

September 5

Read Acts 17:30-31; Matt. 25:31-46; Psa. 98:1-9

As Paul wrapped up his message to the Athenians, he played his ace. The attributes that separate the Unknown God from the false gods are the incarnation and the resurrection. Unlike the many gods of Athens who had never lived in the first place, the Unknown God came to earth as a living, breathing man. He was crucified for our sins and died, but He rose from the dead and will come again to judge all people. The Unknown God is Jesus Christ the Lord. In His grace, God has overlooked much of our ignorance and rebellion. But today God commands all who hear these words to repent. Christ is coming to judge all people. He will separate the sheep from the goats. There will be no middle ground. There will only be the lost and the found, the forgiven and the unforgiven, the saved and the unsaved. Which group will you be in? There is still time to believe. Trust in Jesus!

The Sneering Crowds

September 6

Read Acts 17:32-34; Luke 16:13-15; Luke 23:33-35

The Athenians had been accommodating many gods -- Paul called them to worship only one. Even today, many live with altars to unknown gods in their hearts. Jesus calls us to replace those gods with his Name -- the Name above all names. Christ wants us to know Him personally. Ask the Light of the world to illumine all of the shadowy idols that hinder your relationship with Him. Ask Him to reveal the Unknown God to you. Then, through your life and speech, share Jesus with your family, friends, and neighbors. Just remember… whenever and wherever the truth of Jesus is shared, some will believe, and some will sneer. Some will want to hear more, and some will try to shut you up. We are not called to win the world -- we are to witness to the world. Be faithful, patient, and persistent. Ignore the sneering crowds, and look for those that God has called to new life.

Tent Makers for Jesus

September 7

Read Acts 18:1-3; 1 Corinthians 1:2-6

Paul moved down the road again, ending up in a city called Corinth. We know that he succeeded in planting a church there because we have two letters written to that church in the Bible. While Paul was in Corinth, he met Aquila and Priscilla. They had recently moved from Rome to Corinth, after being expelled by the Emperor Claudius for being Jewish. They could identify with Paul as they shared the common experience of being persecuted and run out of town for your faith. They also connected in that Aquila and Priscilla were tentmakers by trade, as was Paul. This led them to team up in the trade in order to put food on the table while Paul preached the gospel in Corinth. Thus we get the term, "tent making ministry", describing those who work in the marketplace to fund their work in the church. Where there is a will, there is always a way. Use all your gifts to do the work of the Lord.

Preaching Exclusively

September 8

Read Acts 18:4-5; 2 Timothy 4:1-5

When Paul arrived in Corinth, he worked all week making tents and preached every Sabbath. When Silas and Timothy arrived, he was able to return to preaching the word every day. We don't know if they both got jobs to support Paul's ministry, or if they brought an offering along with them from Macedonia. What we do know is that they made it possible for Paul to devote himself full time to preaching and testifying about Christ. This was Paul's passion. Knock him down -- he gets back up. Run him out of one town -- he moves on to the next one. Take away his funding -- he gets a job and preaches whenever he can. There was no stopping this guy! Paul lived to preach that Jesus is Lord. He was also very good at it -- the record speaks for itself. What are you good at? What are you passionate about? Use it to advance the gospel in some way.

When Enough is Enough

September 9

Read Acts 18:6; Matt. 10:12-15; Luke 9:5-6

Sometimes in ministry, we must say, "Enough is enough." Paul shared the gospel with the Jews in Corinth. He argued God's case well, but still they opposed him and would not believe. Finally, Paul threw up his hands and said, "That's enough. I have fulfilled my responsibility to you. I have shared the Good News and you have rejected the truth. I am not responsible for the judgment that awaits you." Some may recoil at the thought of writing anyone off, and certainly we are called to have patience, love, and faith as we pray for and witness to unsaved family, friends, and neighbors. But there comes a time when we must decide how to best spend the limited amount of time and energy we have as a disciple of Jesus. At some point, the Holy Spirit may prompt us to move from the rocky soil, to a more fertile soil. Even Jesus instructed His disciples about this. Pray, and listen for the Lord.

Finding Our Niche

September 10

Read Acts 18:6-8; Isaiah 42:6-7; Gal. 3:8-9

Paul came to a fork in the road, and decided to target a different audience in Corinth. He would take the gospel predominantly to the Gentiles. He had found his niche. He didn't leave town or head for a foreign land -- he went next door. God calls a few to take the gospel across the sea, but all of us are called to take it across the street. Most will never take the gospel overseas, but we can take it to our next door neighbor. We won't be able to look God in the eye and say, "I never had a chance to take the gospel next door." We can never say, "I was too poor to take the gospel across the street." You don't have to be a genius to find your niche. There's a good chance that your "niche" is your neighborhood. Jesus says to all of us, "Take the gospel over there", and our "over there" is very likely next door or across the street. Find your niche. You shouldn't have to look too far.

Conquering the Spirit of Fear

September 11

Read Acts 18:9-11; Luke 12:4-5; 1 Peter 3:13-15

Even apostles need reassurance now and then. How many times must one be beaten up and run out of town before they consider changing their tune? Paul must have been dealing with some fear, because the Lord came to him in a vision, telling him not to be afraid, and to keep on speaking the truth. Paul believed God and obeyed the Lord. He never stopped sharing the gospel, even though he continued to suffer persecution for his faith. He shared Christ boldly wherever he went, at great risk to his personal well being. If we are going to be faithful disciples of Jesus and obey our calling, we too will need to conquer our fears. We must not allow fear to silence us. We must rise above our earthly anxieties. Conquer the spirit of fear that haunts you! Stop running from it. Turn and face it in the name of Jesus. Stare it down with the help of the Holy Spirit. Trust God and walk by faith.

God Keeps His Promise

September 12

Read Acts 18:12-16; Psa. 140:1-5; Psa. 46:10-11

God promised to take care of Paul, and almost immediately Paul was detained and dragged into court by those hostile to the gospel. Paul may have been thinking, "I thought you said you'd take care of me, but here I am in danger again." But before Paul could even open his mouth, the proconsul Gallio dismissed the charges. He told Paul's accusers that he had no time to argue over "questions about words and names", and ejected them from his courtroom. Of course, we know that those "questions about words and names" are life changing and have eternal significance, but on this day God told Paul, "Stand back and watch me move." Paul didn't even have to speak. It would not be his smooth speech that delivered him, but God's Spirit moving on the heart of Gallio. It probably works that way far more often than we know, as God whispers, "Be still and know that I am God."

Religious Thuggery

September 13

Read Acts 18:17; Acts 23:6-10

Religion often turns violent when it is frustrated. Just ask Sosthenes! He had become the new synagogue ruler in Corinth, replacing Crispus, who became a Christian. Sosthenes eventually led an attack on Paul and took him to court, but after the proconsul Gallio dismissed all the charges, the crowd turned on Sosthenes and beat him. Religion often turns on its own when it doesn't get its way. There are no spats as nasty as religious spats. Religious thuggery is never pretty. It destroys the church's moral authority. This is why it's important to move away from "religion" and toward a relationship with Christ. And notice here that Gallio did nothing to intervene. The state does not care if religious people tear each other apart. As the church grows weaker, the state grows stronger. Don't go the way of the Corinthian synagogue. Christ will not bless thuggery in the church.

Strengthening Ministry

September 14

Read Acts 18:18-23; Acts 14:21-22; John 8:31-32

Paul was an evangelist at heart, but knew the importance of strengthening disciples. He gave much of his time to this task. When Paul left Ephesus, he went back to strengthen and disciple believers in those places where he had started churches. Christ's Great Commission calls for the church to teach obedience along with preaching salvation. We must produce followers as well as converts. Teaching people to obey is as important as baptizing them. Discipleship and evangelism are two sides of the same coin. Jesus taught that we can't really be set free by His truth unless we are His disciples. Many today will walk to the front of a church to be saved, but never walk into a classroom of the church to be discipled. The result is biblically illiterate believers with half-baked theology. If you have time for hobbies or recreational activities, you have time for discipleship.

Study the Scriptures

September 15

Read Acts 18:24-25, 28; 2 Peter 1:5-8

Most of us who call ourselves disciples would like to be counted among the faithful who stand up for Jesus. We can learn from Apollos. The Bible says that Apollos was "a learned man with a thorough knowledge of the Scriptures." He had received instruction in the way of the Lord and became a force in the debate in Ephesus about Jesus being the Christ. Before we become teachers, we must become students. To become good teachers, we must first be good learners. God's people have an obligation to know the word of God. We are commanded to add knowledge to our faith. We have been left here on Earth to be change agents for Jesus, and to be effective at this we will have to know more than "Jesus loves me, this I know." That's a great truth, but we will need to go deeper than that if we want to be effective and productive in our knowledge of Christ. Study the Scriptures!

Great Fervor

September 16

Read Acts 18:25; Eph. 3:10; 1 Peter 1:12

Not only did Apollos have a thorough knowledge of the Scriptures, he also taught accurately about the Lord Jesus. Many preachers are steeped in the Scriptures, but their teaching strays from the truth as personal bias creeps in. Not Apollos -- he was a straight arrow. Apollos had another quality that set him apart: he spoke with great fervor. He had more than just "head knowledge". Jesus had moved into his heart and he burned with passion for the gospel. Apollos knew the answer to the greatest question of mankind. He knew the Lord personally and that caused him to enthusiastically proclaim that Jesus is the Answer. He wanted to make the wisdom of God known to everyone. Christians, we have all the tools that Apollos had. We have unlimited access to the Scriptures and to great Bible teachers. If we will supply the great fervor, we too can contribute to changing the world.

The Fear Factor

September 17

Read Acts 18:26; Matthew 10:22-39

We must be people of courage! Jesus spoke of this with His disciples more than once. "Do not be afraid…" is a common phrase in Scripture. Apollos had a "thorough knowledge of the Scriptures", he had the training, and he had a story of faith. But he also had great courage. He had overcome the "fear factor" in ministry. This made him eligible to fill Paul's shoes. He loved God more than anything, even more than life, and so he spoke boldly. He went into the lion's den of the synagogue, and fearlessly proclaimed the truth. He "vigorously refuted" all arguments against Christ. As we've said before in this walk through the book of Acts, this is the missing piece of the puzzle for many Christians today. Too many believers live in fear, not so much for their lives, but for their status among peers. We fear what people will think if we speak of Jesus. Do not be afraid. Trust in God. Speak boldly!

Continuing Education

September 18

Read Acts 18:25-26; Col. 3:16; Prov. 18:15

Even though Apollos was a great preacher and apologist, he was missing one important aspect of the gospel -- he needed some instruction about baptism. Aquila and Priscilla invited Apollos to their home for a meal and some continuing education. This means that this great couple, who had supported Paul, were schooled themselves. They too had a thorough knowledge of Scripture, and had spent some quality time with the apostle Paul in advanced learning. It also means that Apollos had one of the assets necessary to be a great Bible teacher -- he was teachable himself. He didn't think he knew it all. With his level of popularity it would have been easy for him to ignore Priscilla and Aquila. He was drawing big crowds in the synagogue. But he listened to them and learned from them. This is a trait we all need in our walk with Jesus. Christians, we must never stop learning!

Letter of Recommendation

September 19

Read Acts 18:27-28; Romans 16:1-2; 1 Corinthians 4:17; 2 Corinthians 8:16-18

Apollos grew in strength and wisdom, becoming a great apologist for Jesus. God eventually called him to go somewhere else. He had come to Corinth as a "walk on". He left Corinth as an official member of the team, with letters of recommendation from the church. Apollos now had references. This is an important step in becoming a Bible teacher. Seek the blessing of the elders of the church. Don't take off on your own and become a Lone Ranger for the gospel. Anybody with a computer and a blog can claim to be a "Bible teacher" these days. But Apollos submitted himself to the wisdom of the church. He sought their counsel, their blessing, and their endorsement. They responded by writing him reference letters to take with him. If the church watched your walk over a period of time, would they write you a letter of recommendation?

Incomplete Disciples

September 20

Read Acts 19:1-2; 2 Peter 1:3-8

When Paul arrived at Ephesus, he found some disciples. Someone had taken the good news of Jesus there, and a few had put their faith in the Lord. They had accepted God's grace and had become followers of Christ, but there was something missing. Paul asked if they had received the Holy Spirit. They replied that they had never even heard of the Holy Spirit. They had been convicted of their sin and turned to God for forgiveness through Christ, but no one had taught them about God's Holy Spirit. Their faith was not yet complete. There was a page missing from their book. We can be disciples of Jesus, and yet be incomplete. Peter encourages us in Chapter One of his second letter to "make every effort" to add to our faith some qualities that come with the Holy Spirit. Look at his list. Ask the Lord to help you complete your faith and to become more like Jesus every day.

More Than Repentance

September 21

Read Acts 19:3-6; Rom. 8:5; Gal. 5:16-17

The disciples in Ephesus had repented of their sin and been baptized. They were following God to the best of their knowledge. But Paul taught that there is more to being a Christian than just repentance. Christianity is about a new life and a new Spirit. It's about receiving the gift of grace and forgiveness, but also about coming under the Lordship of the Gift Giver. It's about the living Christ moving into our lives and making changes -- changes that we could never make on our own. It's about receiving power for ministry through the Holy Spirit of God, and living by the Spirit rather than by our old nature. It's about receiving spiritual gifts that equip us for ministry. Two spiritual gifts are mentioned in today's verses, but there are many others. Each one is given so that we can serve as a part of Christ's body here on Earth. Discover your gifts and use them to glorify the Lord.

Different Gifts

September 22

Read Acts 19:6; 1 Cor. 12:4-11, 12:28-31, 14:12

God not only saves us, He also gifts us for ministry. These gifts of the Spirit are not a perk -- they are equipment. As the church grew in number, there must have been some confusion about spiritual gifts, for Paul addressed the topic in some of the letters he wrote to churches. Some of the early believers began to focus on certain gifts, making them the litmus test for faith. Paul set them straight. He taught that the gifts of the Spirit are varied, and that God determines which gift(s) each Christian receives. These gifts are given for the common good of the church, not for individual glory. No one receives all the gifts, and there is no one gift that every Christian must receive to substantiate their faith. It is not wrong to desire the "greater" gifts, but we should seek those gifts that benefit the Bride of Christ. The gifts of the Spirit are not for showing off, but for building up the church.

Courage, Discernment, Stamina

September 23

Read Acts 19:8-10; Eph. 5:15-18; Heb. 12:1-4

Paul possessed three traits that are sorely needed in contemporary Christianity: courage, discernment, and stamina. He displayed courage by arguing for Christ under hostile conditions for extended periods of time. He spoke boldly and persuasively for months to obstinate critics who refused to believe, and who maligned Christ. When he discerned that the soil in the synagogue was too rocky, he moved to a local lecture hall and continued daily discussions about the Lord Jesus. We must know when to move on to more fertile soil. Paul preached there for two years -- that's stamina. Many believers today lack persistence. Making disciples takes time. The result of Paul's courage, discernment, and stamina was that "all the Jews and Greeks who lived in the province of Asia heard the word of the Lord." Regardless of what "province" we live in today, that remains a worthy goal.

Power to Restore

September 24

Read Acts 19:11-12; 1 Cor. 2:4-5; 1 Cor. 14:12

When the Holy Spirit comes into our lives, we gain access to the power of God. This power is not just for showing off, but for ministering to others and bringing glory to God. Spiritual gifts are not given so that we can display them like the feathers of a prideful peacock -- they are given so we can display the love of Christ. They are not given for self-promotion, but for ministry to others. They are given so that we can serve. When spiritual gifts are used correctly, healing comes to others -- physical healing, emotional healing, and spiritual healing. The gifts of the Spirit promote wellness in the church. They help build people up, and put people together. When you pray for the gifts of the Spirit, you are praying for the power of God -- power for change, power for witness, power to heal, power to restore, power to make a real difference in this world. Pray for this kind of Holy Spirit power.

Holy Spirit Authority

September 25

Read Acts 19:12; Luke 4:33-37

Power and authority go together. The name of Jesus has power when spoken with authority by Spirit-filled believers. When Christians allow the Spirit to light up and eliminate the evil in their lives, they can then walk and speak with authority to the evil in this world. The Lord's desire is Spirit-filled believers who are not just flashy and loud, but who pack a punch when dealing with the demonic forces here on Earth. We are called to grow to the point that the Holy Spirit's presence in us touches others with God's healing and delivering power -- sometimes just by our mere presence. Desire the gifts of the Spirit, but desire the greater gifts that build up the church and display God's grace and power to this world. Pray for the authority to confront the darkness. Pray for God's love to grow in your heart -- love that serves, and that changes the lives of those you touch.

Risky Business

September 26

Read Acts 19:13-16; Jude 1:8-9

Mouthing off to demonic spirits is risky business, as the seven sons of Sceva discovered in dramatic fashion. These "wannabe" miracle workers hadn't been called by God -- they had called themselves. They presumed upon the power of God. They threw the name of Jesus around like a cheap trinket to impress people, but they did not have God's blessing, nor were they filled with the power of the Holy Spirit. The spirits do not fear boastful people who loudly claim authority over them. They do not fear those who know about Jesus and who spout his name like it was some kind of magical incantation. Never underestimate the power of our enemy. Even the angels know better than to go around mouthing off to demonic spirits. Who the demons really fear is the humble servant of Jesus Christ -- the disciple who is full of God's Spirit, not full of themselves.

The Original Terrorists

September 27

Read Acts 19:16; John 10:10; 1 Peter 5:8

We have an enemy. He goes by many names: Satan, Lucifer, the devil, the evil one. He and his minions are the original terrorists, and they will never change. Their goal is that we have no place where we feel safe and secure from their attacks. Satan and his demons hate us, and just as the seven sons of Sceva discovered, they can overpower us, beat us down, strip us of dignity, and send us running. The devil may tempt us with good things that we crave and covet, but his end goal is not our happiness, or our contentment. His goal is to isolate us, decimate our faith in God, and devour us. He is a liar and a thief, and his intent is to destroy, steal, and kill. Hate, chaos, and carnage are his ultimate delights. Our only hope against his onslaught is to put on the full armor of God and trust in Jesus Christ as Lord and Savior. Only the name of Jesus can defeat these terrorists.

Fear of the Lord

September 28

Read Acts 19:17-18; 2 Corinthians 5:11; 1 Peter 2:17; Revelation 14:6-7

Those living in Ephesus were struck by the power of God. They were in awe of the healing and deliverance Paul did in the name of Jesus. Convicted of their sins, they began to call upon the name of the Lord, proving their repentance by their deeds. Fearing God is not a bad thing. It may have been overdone in days gone by, but many today have gone to the other extreme, reducing God to a harmless do-gooder who loves everything about us. They have made God into a doting grandparent. This is not the God of Scripture. The God of Scripture died on a cross for our sins, but this same God also drowned the Egyptian army in the Red Sea, and consumed the false prophets of Baal with fire from heaven. God is holy and sovereign. He holds the power of life and death, and the keys to heaven and hell. A healthy fear of God is not a bad thing.

Costly Repentance

September 29

Read Acts 19:19-20; 2 Cor. 9:13; Matt. 3:8

When the Ephesians saw the power of God, they responded with a costly repentance. They publicly burned all their expensive sorcery books. Their lives and their values had changed. When was the last time that your relationship with Jesus cost you anything? What have you sacrificed as a result of repentance? Churches today have become adept at touting what they offer to those who attend. Seldom is anyone asked what they have to offer to the church, or told what they must surrender in order to come. We try to make Christianity as easy and as cheap as possible. Costly repentance does not sell very well in a consumer-oriented culture. Advertising benefits will always draw a bigger crowd than calling for sacrifice. But here is the truth: God's grace is offered freely, but following Jesus will always cost you something. Any gospel that tells you otherwise is a false gospel.

The Call to Go

September 30

Read Acts 19:21-22; John 20:19-22; Matt. 10:16-20

Paul was a missionary apostle -- he never stopped thinking about where he should go next to share the gospel and strengthen the church. He wanted to preach in Rome, but first he would return to Jerusalem by way of Macedonia and Achaia. He sent Erastus and Timothy as an advance team to Macedonia, while he stayed in Ephesus a little longer. He had been discipling these two young men, and now he sent them out on the road. When we follow Jesus, he may send us on the road too. He may not send us across the ocean -- our call may be just across the street, or a few miles down the road. But as followers of Jesus, we have all been called to go somewhere, and if we never go anywhere with the gospel, perhaps it is not Jesus we are following. Christ's call is to go into all the world and make disciples. Near or far, let Jesus direct your steps as you obey His call.

The Disturbing People of the Way

October 1

Read Acts 19:23; Acts 4:1-4; Matt. 2:1-3

The early church had been derisively called "Christians" at Antioch. In Ephesus someone decided to label them as "The Way". Both labels were meant to be derogatory. Wherever those early disciples lived, they caused a disturbance as they lived out their faith. As others became believers, their lifestyle and spending habits changed. They were rocking the boat, messing with the system, stirring the pot, and this caused friction. They didn't fit the mold, and what they had seemed to be contagious. They disturbed the status quo. Contrast that with many church people today, whose main goal seems to be blending in. We wouldn't want anyone to think we are weird, and so we become adept at flying under the radar. Something has been lost in the translation. We were saved to shine! Live out your faith, and pray that you can become part of the disturbance in a way that honors the Lord.

A Different Kind of Buyer

October 2

Read Acts 19:24-26; Matt. 6:19-24

As more and more people in Ephesus were saved, a recession hit the idol making business. Paul taught that the silver idols of Artemis had no divine power, and people stopped spending money on them. Demetrius called the union bosses together and launched a public relations campaign against the Church. These new believers, led by Paul, were cutting into the idol-maker's profits. They were taking their faith too seriously, and it was harming the local economy. These new people of the Way had changed their spending habits and had become a different kind of buyer. Every Christian should be a different kind of buyer. Money that was once spent foolishly will now be offered to Jesus, or wisely saved for future needs. If your God has not affected the way you spend money, your God is not the God of Scripture. Becoming a disciple of Jesus will make you a different kind of buyer.

Led Astray

October 3

Read Acts 19:26; Matthew 7:13-14

Anyone who takes their Christian faith seriously will begin to walk a different road than the rest of the world. In turn, popular culture will see you as "off the beaten path" or even as "off your rocker". Christians have been labeled as "wacko" since the days of Jesus. If you haven't been called a "wacko" or something worse, you have likely been hiding your light. Demetrius and the other establishment idol-makers saw the early believers as people who had been "led astray". The "folly" of this new religious sect was found in their rejection of "man-made gods". Those on the wide road to destruction cannot comprehend why disciples of Jesus persist in going a different direction, but we who follow Jesus have been commanded to walk the narrow road. If we obey, we are indeed guilty of "straying" from the wide road. We must learn to live with the world's ridicule and disdain.

The Gods of Culture

October 4

Read Acts 19:26-29; 2 Cor. 4:3-4; Deut. 4:23-29

Many today would say they are not religious, but they are not being truthful. We are all religious in some way. We all worship something or someone. Some worship science. Some worship nature. Some worship the stars. Some worship money. Some worship sex. Some worship power. Some worship sports. Some worship their addiction. Some worship themselves. The gods of culture are many, and if you faithfully follow Jesus, you will come into conflict with these gods. As the influence of Christ grows in your life, the power of cultural gods will begin to wane. They will begin to get less of your time and money, and they will squeal their displeasure. They may even threaten you. The gods of the culture despise Jesus and those who serve Him, but remain steadfast. Those who worship the gods of culture will perish, while those who follow Jesus receive eternal life.

Chaos Reigns

October 5

Read Acts 19:29-32; Rom. 1:18-23, 28-31

The God of Scripture is a God of order. Chaos is of the devil. Mob violence is evil -- it is not of God. Where people are in an uproar and rush as one man to ruthlessly destroy and do senseless harm, Satan has taken control. When people reject divine guidance, one finds heartless depravity, futile thinking, and confusion about purpose and direction. Chaos reigns, and we end up not even knowing why we are here. This can happen with crowds, and with individuals. God offers peace and light, but we are addicted to chaos and darkness. We turn away from God, and then can't figure out why our lives are so disordered and empty. We worship false gods, and our main purpose in life becomes survival. There is a better way. Jesus offers peace and light in the place of calamity and darkness. Let Christ reign instead of chaos. Embrace Jesus and be set free. Our God reigns!

Religious Competition

October 6

Read Acts 19:33-34; Matthew 24:7-14

When religion drives the hearts of people and their economy, it will not tolerate dissent. It is easier to eliminate those who challenge the system than to compete in the marketplace of ideas. Mob violence becomes a standard response. We see it here in the near-death experience of Paul and his friends in Ephesus. We see it in the killing of Jesus, and in the angry crowd surrounding the cross. We see it in our world today in the public beheadings of those considered infidels, and in the sinister character assassination of anyone foolish enough to challenge the secular gods of political correctness. Even Christianity, when twisted just a bit, can become a toxic religion that burns heretics at the stake, and drowns those suspected of witchcraft. This is not the way of Jesus! He offers love, and heals hearts with grace and forgiveness. We should do the same.

Grace Out of Darkness

October 7

Read Acts 19:35; Ephesians 2:1-9

One of the greatest truths of Scripture comes from Paul's letter to the Ephesians. We are saved by grace through faith, not by our works. This "amazing grace" letter becomes even more significant when you consider that Ephesus was a very dark and idolatrous city. The Temple of Artemis was huge and ornate. It was one of the Seven Wonders of the Ancient World. The worship of Artemis was sophisticated, upscale idolatry, but idolatry nonetheless. Those who worshipped at her altar were part of the darkness. They were even willing to kill for her, as evidenced by the mob that went after Paul. But God poured out His grace at Ephesus -- people were saved, and a church grew there. The love of God overcomes the hate of the world. Light dispels darkness. Darkness may despise the light, but the light continues to shine. This is our calling as disciples of Jesus. Shine!

Responsible Government

October 8

Read Acts 19:36-41; Rom. 13:1-7; Matt. 22:21

The God of Scripture is a God of order, not chaos. The mob mentality seen in Acts 19 and that we see on our news broadcasts, is not of God. Responsible government will favor order over chaos, but remain neutral regarding the establishment of religion. The city clerk in Ephesus reminded the mob that it was not the government's business to judge one religion as better than another. Government's role is to protect and maintain order. He told them that if laws had been broken, the offenders could be taken to court in an orderly fashion. But the government would not punish people just for having a different religion, nor would it allow any kind of rioting or mob action. Good government will not legislate or mandate religious beliefs. It will not bless a particular religion, nor will it display hostility toward religion. Instead it will protect and work for the good of all.

Encouraging Words

October 9

Read Acts 20:1-2; Rom. 15:4-6; Heb. 3:13

Paul was an exhorter, a great public speaker, and a devastating debater. Many of Paul's messages and letters were confrontational in nature, so we can get this image of him as a negative kind of guy who was always on somebody's case about something. But Paul also had a positive side. You didn't want him on your case, but you were definitely blessed to have him on your side. As he returned to some of the churches that he had planted, he encouraged them. There is a fine line between exhortation and encouragement, but we need both at times. There are so many things in this world that tear us down. We all need someone who will build us up with encouraging words and exhort us to keep going. When was the last time you encouraged anyone inside or outside the church? Be an encourager in someone's life. Make that call. Write that note. Just do it.

A Dangerous Way

October 10

Read Acts 20:2-3; Matthew 12:9-16

Everywhere Paul went, people were saved and churches were started. But everywhere Paul went, he also faced plots against his life. He faced this stressful dilemma on a daily basis. His steps were ordained by God, but his way was continuously dangerous. If we share the gospel, our road will also be dangerous. There will be some who plot to do us harm. As a result, many Christians try to remain anonymous. If God gave awards for flying under the radar, many in the church would have a full trophy case. How else can one explain the fact that most believers quake in their boots at the thought of witnessing, and have never led another person to Jesus Christ? It is good that Paul and the other apostles were not like this, or Christianity would have died as an infant in Jerusalem. The Jesus way can certainly be dangerous, but it is our glorious calling to walk in it.

Second Generation Honor Roll

October 11

Read Acts 20:4-6; Acts 6:7; Luke 10:1-3

A few chapters ago in Acts, it was just Silas walking with Paul. Now the one has become seven. Not only are more and more people being saved, more are serving as ministers with Paul. This list of names is like an "honor roll" of second generation apostles -- men who had never personally seen Jesus, but who laid their lives on the line and who had the faith to preach the gospel. Some of these names are never mentioned again in Scripture, but are immortalized here. We don't know their fate, but it's likely that some gave their very lives as heroes for Christ. That raises a question. If you had lived during this time would your name have made it into the Book? When you are gone, will your name be remembered for your exceptional service to the church? Serve in such a way as to earn a place with those at the honors banquet on the other side. You won't be sorry you did.

Dangerous Dozing in Church

October 12

Read Acts 20:6-12; Luke 8:49-55; 1 Thess. 5:3-9

When Paul preached at a Sunday night service in Troas, they didn't get the "Reader's Digest" version -- they got the full unabridged novel. Paul preached "on and on". He was leaving the next day and wanted to share everything he could about Jesus. Around midnight, a young man who was sitting in the third-story window, fell asleep and was killed when he fell to the ground. Paul went down, prayed life back into him, then went back upstairs and preached until daybreak. It's amazing what someone rising from the dead can do. That's still true today. Dozing off in church can be dangerous. It can even cause death. Here, the death of Eutychus -- today, the death of one's faith. When we sleep in the presence of God's word long enough, we can eventually stop hearing, lose spiritual consciousness, and suffer a serious fall. Keep your eyes open, and remain alert.

Sleeping With Eyes Open

October 13

Read Acts 20:9; Rom. 13:11-14; Rev. 3:1-3

There are some today like this young man who fell asleep, tumbled from a third-story window, hit the ground, and died. They have been asleep and have fallen hard. They are part of the living dead and need a resurrection. They need Jesus to breathe life into them, or they will be lost forever. But there are also many in the church today who are sleeping with their eyes open. They have received that touch from Jesus, and they have the appearance of being awake, but they are asleep in the light. Jesus may have opened their eyes once, but their ears and their hearts have been disengaged for years. They no longer hear the word of the Lord. They no longer see His glory. They no longer feel the Spirit moving. If this describes you -- if you were alive to Christ once, but have been sleeping in church with your eyes open, God says, "Wake up!" Spiritual sleep walking is dangerous. Wake up!

Living Consistently

October 14

Read Acts 20:13-18; 1 Cor. 15:58; Gal. 6:9

In good times and bad, Paul stayed the course, and modeled for us what it means to be a faithful servant of the Lord. One of the marks of a faithful disciple is consistency. When the elders of Ephesus came to see Paul, he boldly told them to consider his life as evidence for the grace and power of God. He basically said, "Look at how I have lived among you. My life is an open book. I have lived consistently. I am proof that Jesus lives, because you can see how He lives in me." Could you say that? Are you confident that if someone watched how you live on a daily basis, they would see what it means to live like Jesus? Could anyone see Jesus through the consistency of your life witness? If not, what is it that blurs the image of Christ in your life? What is causing your witness to be sporadic rather than consistent? There is where change must begin. Ask God to start there.

Humility

October 15

Read Acts 20:19; Phil. 2:3; Col. 3:12; James 3:13

Pride is a church killer. It has been called "the deadliest sin". It is certainly at the root of many other sins. Pride can cause us to look down on others, and to think we ought to be in a higher position than we are. It can draw us into thinking that we have not received the respect due to us -- that we deserve much better than what we have now. If anyone had reason for pride, it was Paul. His credentials were second to none, and his record of service was exemplary. But he was a humble man. He knew where his blessing and authority came from. He knew that whatever he received, it was better than he deserved. Is that how you think? Are you genuinely humble, or has pride crept into your life like a cancer? Maybe it's time to get off the high horse and assume a kneeling position. Ask God to cut away the pride in your life, but don't expect it to be a pleasant experience.

Enduring Service

October 16

Read Acts 20:19; Acts 20:23; 2 Cor. 6:3-10

Paul was "severely tested", even to the point of tears. God told him that he would suffer, yet he forged ahead. He endured beatings, prison, hunger, pain, and other hardships, but his love for Jesus and his calling to preach the gospel just got stronger. When things got tough, Paul endured. Genuine disciples expect some pain and difficulty. They work through adversity, rather than being defeated by it. They expect the road to be rough, and yet they press on. This is our calling. Tune out those teachers who promise unending spiritual bliss if you buy their book and follow their advice. That is unbiblical teaching. Every true disciple will endure some hardship and pain. Stop whining and start working! Consider those who've gone ahead of you and who've suffered greatly for the cause of Christ. Draw strength from their example. Accept what comes, and give glory to God.

Double Barreled Witness

October 17

Read Acts 20:20; Acts 5:41-42; Eph. 4:15

Paul was a double barreled witness and preacher. He never hesitated to speak what he thought would be helpful to those listening. He preached the truth in love -- a double-barreled combination that's hard to beat. Paul also had a double barreled method of witnessing and preaching. He took the gospel into the public square, sharing Jesus with the crowds. But Paul also took the gospel from house to house. He spent time in homes, sharing the truth about Jesus. This is a great lesson for us. It's good to invite people to church. Every Christian should be an inviter. We should be willing to witness in public -- on street corners, at Wal-Mart, at the lake, or at the ballgame. But it is also effective to invite people to your home, or to go to their homes, and share the truth of Jesus with them. It's the double-barreled, public and private approach of Paul, and it is still effective today.

Double-Barreled Message

October 18

Read Acts 20:21; Rom. 3:21-24; 2 Peter 3:9

Paul had a double-barreled method -- he shared Jesus in public places and in private homes. He had a double-barreled audience -- he shared the gospel with both Jews and Gentiles. Paul also had a double-barreled message -- turn to God in repentance, and have faith in the Lord Jesus Christ. Repentance is more than being sorry for our sins -- it is a willingness to turn away from sin, and turn toward Christ. Who we turn toward is as important as what we turn away from. The gospel is accessed through repentance, and is completed with faith in Jesus. If our faith is not in Christ, we do not have a Christian faith. Jesus loves us. Jesus died for us. Jesus rose for us. Jesus calls to us. Jesus saves us. Jesus walks with us. Is your faith in Him? This is the double-barreled message that Paul preached: earnestly repent of sin, and in faith, sincerely turn to Christ. Is this the gospel you have believed?

Radical Single-Minded Mission

October 19

Read Acts 20:22-24; 1 Cor. 9:16; 2 Tim. 4:6-8

Paul had a double-barreled message and a double-barreled method, but he was single-minded in his mission. Compelled by the Spirit to preach the gospel, he was determined to finish the race and complete the task Christ had given him. He considered his life worth nothing, laying it on the line daily as he testified to the gospel of grace. He was consumed with completing his mission. He could not focus on anything else. Paul sacrificed his life for the sake of his calling. He was a radical for Jesus. Are you a radical? The word "radical" has taken on a negative connotation today, but most of the world's great people were radical in their vision, their approach, and their sacrifice. Are you willing to consider your life worth nothing to yourself? Do you feel compelled, no matter what the cost, to testify to the gospel of grace? If so, then you could become a single-minded radical for Jesus.

Innocent of the Blood

October 20

Read Acts 20:26; Psalm 19:9-14

Paul testified that he was innocent of the blood of all men. But before he became a believer, Paul had incited violence against the church and stood in approval of Stephen's stoning. So when Paul says he is "innocent of the blood of all men", he must be speaking spiritually. He was saying that when he stood before God, he would never be accused of not trying to lead people to Jesus. He did his best to persuade everyone to be saved. If they refused to believe, their blood would be on their own hands. Paul would be found "innocent of the blood of all men" because he shared the gospel with everyone he came into contact with. He preached salvation by grace through faith everywhere he went. Can you say that? This world would be a much different place if all Christians could stand before God and honestly declare along with Paul, "I am innocent of the blood of all men."

No Hesitation

October 21

Read Acts 20:27; 2 Peter 3:9; John 3:16

God's will for those who are lost is that they be found. God does not want anyone to perish. He sent His Son Jesus to rescue us. God gave the life of His Son so that we could be found -- so that we could have life. Jesus died to pay for our sin. This provides all people with the opportunity to obtain eternal life. The Holy Spirit convicts us of our sin, providing both the awareness of being lost, as well as the desire for rescue. But the lost must hear the truth, and we who have believed are the truth-tellers. We have been called to provide the proclamation and the witness -- our lives, our words, laid out for the glory of God. The church is God's rescue team — sent out to proclaim the gospel. As Paul neared the end of his life, he could say with integrity, "I have held nothing back." Will you be able to say that? Paul had not hesitated to proclaim the whole will of God -- neither should we!

Shepherds of the Church

October 22

Read Acts 20:28-29; Matt. 10:16-20; 1 Peter 5:1-11

Paul and Peter called on elders to protect their flocks, but every disciple of Jesus should be prepared to help with this. Paul tells them to "keep watch" over themselves. You cannot lead others to Jesus if you yourself are not being led by Jesus. You cannot teach what you have not learned. Do what it takes to get strong and stay strong. God has called us to defend His sheep against "savage wolves". The battle is not over just because we said the "sinner's prayer" one Sunday. Believers will be attacked by the Enemy. Satan is like a roaring lion who roams the Earth looking for someone to devour. That someone may be your child, your mate, your friend, or your neighbor. Are you prepared to take on the wolves and lions, or will you tuck tail and run when you hear their snarls? Put on the armor of God. Be ready to fight the good fight. With training, we can all help protect the flock.

The Enemy Within

October 23

Read Acts 20:30-31; 2 Peter 2:1-3

Paul the apostle understood human nature. He knew that there would always be some who were more interested in having a following, than in doing the following. They would be far more interested in gathering disciples than in making disciples. It's an ego thing, and it's always divisive and harmful. Some people just have the need to control others, and they will even distort the truth (which is lying) in order to gain influence and exert power. Watch out for these false teachers, but moreover, be careful you don't become one of them. Most of us need correction at times. Be honest about your errors and failings. Do what it takes to correct your course… if you are off course and have followers, then they are off course too, and you are responsible for their souls. So watch yourself, and be on guard. Heed Paul's warning. Keep your eyes on Jesus and not the crowd.

Grace and Holiness

October 24

Read Acts 20:32; Rom. 15:15-16; 1 Cor. 1:2-4

Paul speaks here of receiving sanctification through being built up in the word of God's grace. Sanctification is being made holy. Sanctification and holiness are interchangeable words. We are sanctified by the Holy Spirit when we are saved by grace, through faith. But then we are called by God to grow in grace -- to grow in holiness. This takes effort on our part. Many today want God's grace, but balk at doing the work of pursuing holiness. We want the inheritance that God promises, without having to be in a relationship that changes our lives. We want the benefits of sanctification, without the discipline of living a life apart from sin. We can never achieve perfection here on Earth, but we should strive toward holiness as we endeavor to live a life that is pleasing to God. We are called to become more and more like our Master as we daily grow in grace and holiness.

Grace and Giving

October 25

Read Acts 20:33-35; Mark 10:17-23; 2 Cor. 8:1-7

Paul calls the Ephesians to display a proper attitude toward money and possessions. We would be wise to hear his call as well. Resist the covetousness that is prevalent in modern culture. It is the tap root of greed, envy, and theft. The silver, gold, and clothing of others is of no interest to those living in God's Kingdom. We are called to work for our daily bread. By the grace of God, our hands supply our own needs, and the needs of others. Kingdom people are giving people, not taking people. The sense of entitlement we see today is a product of living on the wide road to destruction. Those on the narrow road that leads to life, will excel in the grace of giving. Seeking treasure in heaven, they will be richly generous with ministry and money. They know that more blessing is found in giving than in receiving. This was the attitude of Jesus. Is it your attitude?

The Sting of Love

October 26

Read Acts 20:25, 36-38; Matthew 16:21-25

As Paul prepared to leave for Jerusalem, he dropped a bombshell -- he told his friends that he would never see them again. There were tears, hugs, and kisses, but they knew these were not just idle words. Love is a double-edged sword. It is great to love and be loved, but love causes pain when it comes time to part ways. If we truly love, we will eventually weep, because nothing lasts forever here on Earth. There will come a day when we see those loved ones for a final time on this side of eternity, and that can cause deep anguish. But we should still love! We should love each other so much that it hurts to say goodbye. We should love people in such a way that it is painful to lose them -- or for them to lose us. How many will shed tears when you depart? We should live and love in a way that causes that number to continuously grow. Love can sting, but it is well worth the pain.

A Face Like Flint

October 27

Read Acts 21:1-6; Acts 21:10-12; Isaiah 50:7

The prophet Isaiah once said that he had set his face like flint and would not be disgraced. Today we see Paul ignore the pleadings of friends, set his face like flint, and head for Jerusalem. The prophet Agabus warned Paul that he would be bound and imprisoned by the Gentiles. But Paul already knew that "prison and hardships" faced him wherever he went (Acts 20:23). He had looked death in the face several times and not flinched. He had counted the cost and was willing to pay it. Paul went to Jerusalem with full knowledge of what awaited him there. The counsel of friends and family can be good, but often they love us more than they love God, and they want us to love them more than we love God. They worry more about our personal safety than about the mission God has given us. Paul's friends forgot that he loved Jesus more than he loved his life. We are called to that same love!

Growing the Church

October 28

Read Acts 21:4; Acts 21:7-8; Acts 16:5

Paul and his fellow workers had scattered seeds of the gospel all around the Mediterranean Sea, and those seeds had taken root and grown. When Paul began he was the first Christian to enter many cities. But as he headed back to Jerusalem, he found Christians almost everywhere. The infant church was reproducing itself. When Paul reached Caesarea, he stayed at the house of Philip, who was one of the seven men chosen to run the church's feeding program for widows and orphans back in Acts, Chapter 6. Phillip had compassion gifts, and had been called to a "hands on" service ministry. But Phillip had other gifts as well. This man who waited on tables had also been given the gift of evangelism, and led many to Christ. What are your gifts? You likely have more than one. Be sure to discover them and use them for the glory of God. It's both our privilege and our calling.

Phillip's Four Gifts

October 29

Read Acts 21:9; Luke 2:36-38; Judges 4:4-5

God had given Phillip gifts of compassion and evangelism, but he had also received four other gifts from the Lord. Phillip had been given four daughters with prophetic gifts. The biblical gift of prophecy is not just about seeing the future. Those with prophetic gifts have the ability to speak the word of God into the lives of others in a way that brings conviction and change. These four women had been given the gift of preaching God's word with power. Many have strong feelings about women in ministry, but what is clear is that these four women, along with others in Scripture, had prophetic gifting. It is also obvious that Phillip had not kept them locked up in a closet. They had been using their gifts, prophesying in their community. God does not give us gifts just so we can say we have them. God gives men and women gifts to use for the glory of His kingdom. Use yours!

Ready to Die for Jesus

October 30

***Read Acts 21:13-15; Acts 20:24;
Luke 9:23-24; Revelation 12:11***

Paul was ready and willing to die for Jesus, but he had really died on that road to Damascus years earlier. He had died to himself and had become a new man. God had placed him on a different road. His life had changed course, and staying alive was no longer his chief concern. Death no longer held sway over him. Paul did not die in Jerusalem, as his friends feared, but was taken prisoner and shipped to Rome, where he was martyred for his faith. But he was prepared because he had settled the issue of what he was willing to die for. He had decided that he was willing to die for the gospel of Jesus. In his heart of hearts, Paul counted his life worth nothing to himself, and laid it down for Christ. He was willing to carry the cross, even if it led to his death. How about you? Have you decided what you are willing to die for?

Living for Jesus

October 31

***Read Acts 20:22; Romans 14:8;
2 Corinthians 5:14-15; Galatians 2:19-20***

As he set out for Jerusalem, Paul was willing to die for Jesus. Down through the centuries, many have been willing to do the same. Not every Christian will be called upon to die for Jesus, but every Christian is called to live for Jesus! And living for Jesus may prove to be as difficult as dying for Jesus -- perhaps even more difficult. If it is not more difficult, then why do so many Christians today find it nearly impossible to do? Why is it so hard to live fully for Christ? Why is it so difficult to sell out completely to the Lord -- to share the gospel with our lives and our words, regardless of the consequences? Perhaps we are not yet "compelled" by the same Spirit as Paul was. He was not chomping at the bit to die for Jesus, but he was compelled to live for Christ. The rest was up to the Lord. Do you feel compelled to live for Jesus today? Will you?

The Down Side of Denominations

November 1

Read Acts 21:17-26; Galatians 3:28

When Paul arrived in Jerusalem, he went to James and the elders of the church to report on his ministry among the Gentiles. They praised God, but there was a problem. The church in Jerusalem had also been growing, and they were insistent that the Law of Moses should be observed. This differed from Paul's teaching that circumcision was no longer needed for one to be obedient to God, and that salvation was by faith alone. This may be the first denominational disagreement. The Jewish Church and the Gentile Christians worshipped the same Jesus, but they practiced their faith differently. Some just cannot seem to get by this. This is the downside of denominations. Rather than focusing on our commonality in Christ, we tend to dwell on our differences and diminish those who are different. Be cautious! This does not usually end up advancing the Kingdom of God.

Religious Persecution

November 2

Read Acts 21:27-28; Acts 13:45-52; Acts 14:1-7

Many Christians today think atheism is a great danger, but throughout the ages, the presence of religion has stirred persecution more than the absence of religion. Religion has tortured and killed more Christians than atheism. Religion persecutes those who think differently. It never works alone. It stirs up the crowd. It has to have a following. It has to be in control. Religion can't function unless someone is obeying rules. That's why it can justify using intimidation and beatings to force submission. Religion is more about hoarding followers than about following Jesus. It's more about corporate compliance than personal piety. It doesn't care about what's in your heart -- it cares about how you behave on the outside. It sees going through the motions as a good thing, and highly values everyone looking and acting the same. Beware of the "groupthink" that comes with religion.

People, Practices, Positions, Places

November 3

Read Acts 21:28; Acts 6:9-15

Religion enshrines people, practices, positions, and places, and attacks anyone who seemingly denigrates any of these four things. Paul wasn't teaching against the faith he grew up in, he was teaching against the religion it had become -- a religion that enslaved people instead of freeing them. When people get religious, their gurus become infallible, their practices become required, their doctrinal positions become the voice of God, and their buildings become shrines. So we get holy mountains, holy men, holy temples, holy water, holy ground, holy smoke, holy cities, and the holy land -- yet our hearts remain sinful and empty. Salvation is not based on people, practices, positions, or places. It is based on the Prince of Peace. We must be careful not to elevate people, practices, places, or positions to the place where only God should be. If we do, we have become idolaters.

Unfit for the Kingdom

November 4

Read Acts 21:28-29; Matt. 9:10-13; Matt. 21:28-32

Paul was accused of defiling the temple area by bringing a Greek there. Greeks were considered unfit to enter the holy places of the Jews. This is another negative aspect of religion -- it declares certain people to be unfit for the Kingdom. The Jews didn't think Greeks were fit to be near God. Jesus was also criticized for hanging around with hookers, lepers, and tax collectors, all of whom the religionists had declared unfit for God. The Lord would never come near or speak to people like these. This is what religion does -- it categorizes, separates, and judges. It declares some people unfit for the church. We must guard against adopting these same religious attitudes. Jesus came to save sinners. No one is unfit for the Kingdom until God pronounces judgment on the last day. Do not partner with a religion that declares some to be unfit for God's mercy. That mindset is not of Christ.

Religious Chaos

November 5

Read Acts 21:30-31; Acts 19:24-32; Matt. 27:17-26

Religion promises order, but generally ends up delivering chaos. The Jews in the days of Christ and the early church were some of the most religious people in the history of the world, but they were continually at the center of chaos and disorder. Religion often divides more than it unites. It can bring the illusion of peace and order through coercion and intimidation, but it is actually not that much different than the Pax Romana which the Jewish people lived under in the days of Christ. Religion cannot bring peace any more than Roman rule brought peace. They offered a semblance of order, but ruled with an iron fist. It was a peace enforced by the sword and spear. It was a fear-induced peace, not the peace of God. Only Jesus can bring true peace and order as God's Holy Spirit works from the inside out. Seek God's peace, not the peace promised by world governments.

What Goes Around

November 6

Read Acts 21:31-36; Acts 7:51-58; Mark 15:9-15

"What goes around comes around." seemed to be playing itself out in Paul's life. He had been a persecutor, and supervised the mob action that took Stephen's life. Now his life was in danger for his faith in Christ. But rather than being "bad karma", this incident simply illustrates how far some religions will go to eliminate the competition. It happened to Jesus as the mob shouted, "Crucify Him!" It happened to Paul as the crowd yelled, "Away with him!" And we see it happening today as people are shot, hung, drowned, and burned alive for not believing the same way that those in power believe. It's an age old problem and symptomatic of a religious cancer that plagues mankind. There are those who really believe their religion can be furthered by hating and killing those who don't believe like them. This is not the Jesus way. Love, not hate, is Christ's way of changing the world.

A Powerful Testimony

November 7

Read Acts 21:37-40; Acts 22:1-5

Once again, under difficult circumstances, Paul shares his personal testimony. Paul's testimony serves as a model for us. A powerful testimony speaks in a language people can understand -- a language that quiets people and causes them to listen. It's ironic, but the longer we are in the church, the greater is the danger that we will begin to speak a language which is foreign to the lost. We can begin to speak "Church-ese", a language laced with big words that the unsaved ear cannot comprehend. Work at keeping it simple. A powerful testimony also deals honestly with our past. Paul didn't whitewash his past, but neither did he come across as the worst sinner ever to live. He didn't boast of his badness. He shared the truth, without all the dirty details. People don't need to hear every page in your diary to know that you were a sinner. Be honest, but get to the good news as soon as possible.

I Am Jesus

November 8

Read Acts 22:6-10; Exodus 3:13-16

Paul never forgot the misdeeds of his past. Most of us can identify. But he also never forgot the day he met Jesus. It was the defining moment in his life. You don't come face to face with the great I Am and not remember it. It wasn't a pleasant moment, but it was a blessed moment. Paul was knocked to the ground and blinded by one who said, "I Am Jesus.", and then lifted up and given eyes to see by the mercy and grace of our Lord. How we met Jesus is a crucial part of every Christian's story. Think about it… when you think of Paul, what comes to your mind? Do you think persecutor/murderer? No! You think Damascus Road. Culture even uses the term "Damascus Road Experience" to describe a dramatic turn-around in a person's life. We would do well to spend less time remembering how bad we were, and more time testifying to the life change that came when we met Jesus.

Helping Hands

November 9

Read Acts 22:11-14; Jeremiah 29:11-13

In our faith journey, many of us have had companions who led us when we couldn't see well. We've had those special people that God sent at just the right time to speak truth, hope, and sometimes conviction into our lives. Ananias came to Paul at just the right time and provided God's hand of healing and voice of calling. He gave Paul a hope and a future. There were others who showed Jesus to Paul, and who helped him grow and mature. He mentions some of them by name in his letters. When you share your story, tell about what Jesus has done for you through others since he lifted you up. You can share it without being proud or boastful. Thank those people who have helped you. Build them up. This cruel and harsh world will take care of tearing them down and humbling them. Let others know what they've meant to you, as you give glory to God for your growth.

Rid the Earth of Him

November 10

Read Acts 22:14-22; Luke 4:24-30

Like Paul, we who believe have been chosen to know God's will, and to speak the truth of Jesus. Our life's purpose has changed. We have been chosen to have our sins washed away and to hear the words of God. We've been called to go to those in need of God's grace. We've been commanded to love them and to share the story of God's mercy. We will not always be well received or popular with the crowds. Many do not want to hear that God has mercy on the lost, the unclean, the hookers, the homeless, and the hated. Many do not want to hear that God has called us to repent and turn from sin. Some may turn on you and try to shout you down. Enemies of Christ's name will judge you unfit to live and try to rid the Earth of you. But we have this calling, so tell the truth anyway. Be honest about your past, but also speak of the changes that have come through Jesus. Be His witness!

Citizenship Matters

November 11

Read Acts 22:22-25; Eph. 2:11-13

Citizenship matters -- or at least it should! What many take for granted, others will risk death to obtain. It is that way with nations, and it should be that way with the Kingdom of God. Before we came to Christ, we were aliens to the Kingdom. We were outsiders. We were foreigners without hope. Then we became citizens of God's kingdom, and when we did, we obtained not just the privileges of citizenship, but also the responsibilities of citizenship. We were no longer aliens. Once we lived far away, but then we were brought near. We found a new home. We began to learn a new language. We adopted the laws of the Kingdom as our own. People we formerly had no relationship with became like brothers and sisters to us. We began to behave as if we belonged, because our relationship had changed. We began to behave responsibly. Citizenship matters -- or at least it should!

Transferred Loyalty

November 12

Read Acts 22:26-27; Philippians 3:18-20

A naturalized citizen has transferred their loyalty from one nation to another. In the past, the USA was a "melting pot". People came from all over and melted together as citizens of one nation. Today, citizenship has been cheapened, and the nation is more like a "salad bowl" than a melting pot. Individualism reigns supreme. Assimilation is no longer necessary. Allegiance is no longer required, and loyalty has diminished. The same thing has happened in much of the church. We invite people to come join us, but "come as you are" has morphed into "remain as you are". No change is required. No melting is necessary -- that would require heat, and we want to be seen as "cool". Our Jesus offers a lot and demands very little. But this is not the Jesus or the church of Scripture. Citizenship in God's Kingdom has requirements, discipleship is costly, and Christ commands a non-negotiable transfer of loyalty.

Becoming a Citizen

November 13

Read Acts 22:28; Ephesians 2:13-20

Many of us were born citizens of our nation. We didn't have to do anything. Perhaps that is why so many take their freedoms and privileges for granted. But for many, a citizen is something you must become. There are classes to take and oaths to swear. They must renounce all other allegiances, and swear to support, defend, and serve the nation. It works that way with God's Kingdom. We aren't born citizens, nor can we buy our citizenship. Someone else already bought it for us. His name is Jesus, and we are called to covenant with Him, renouncing all other allegiances, and promising our support and service. Many Christians neglect this today. We desire the privileges of citizenship, but reject the loyalty and the service. This produces a weak and self-serving church. God is looking for some people who will transfer their loyalty and become citizens of His Kingdom. Can He count on you?

No More Chains

November 14

Read Acts 22:29; Luke 4:18; Psa. 116:16; Gal. 5:1

In most nations, citizens have rights that non-citizens do not have. The Roman commander knew that he was not allowed to put a Roman citizen in chains without good cause. Citizens have rights. We who are citizens of the Kingdom also do not belong in chains. Jesus came to set us free, but many Christians remain in bondage. Their chains are not visible, but they are real. They are in bondage to regret, bitterness, anxiety, abuse, addiction, envy, un-forgiveness, and many other maladies. If you are a citizen of God's Kingdom and still in chains, it is not something God has willed. You may not have chosen your particular chains in the beginning, but you do have a choice about remaining in them. Do you want to be free? Jesus came to proclaim freedom for the prisoners! Cry out to Him, and when the chains fall off, do not return to them again. A citizen does not belong in chains.

Fulfilling Our Duty

November 15

Read Acts 22:30; Acts 23:1; Romans 15:15-17; Ecclesiastes 12:13-14

On what could have easily been the last day of his life, Paul looked the religious stuffed shirts of his day in the eye, and told them his conscience was clear. He had fulfilled his priestly duty to God. He had been called by God to proclaim the gospel and that's what he was doing. He had answered God's call with zeal and would make no apologies for it. Could you say that today? Could you look a hostile crowd (or any crowd) in the eye and say, "I have fulfilled my duty to God in all good conscience."? Could you look Jesus in the eye and say that? If not, why not? What is holding you back? What is preventing you from fulfilling your duty to God? Maybe it's time to clean house. Perhaps serving Jesus should become a higher priority on your schedule. He certainly didn't die on the cross to play second fiddle. Fulfill your duty to the Lord.

Fully Obeying God

November 16

Read Acts 23:2-5; John 5:39-40; 2 Tim. 3:16-17

Paul was right in objecting to being hit in the mouth. Defendants had rights under Jewish law. Ananias was wrong. He violated God's law by ordering that Paul be struck. But Paul was also wrong because he spoke rashly and harshly -- something that is almost always counter-productive. He did not realize that Ananias was the High Priest. Paul knew the Scriptures well, and he quoted Exodus 22:28. He had violated this commandment and apologized to Ananias and the court for his words. Paul demonstrates here that it's never proper to break God's law just because someone else does. After his outburst, he showed a spirit of humility and obedience in his apology. All Scripture is given to us by God, and should be taken seriously by those who love Jesus. We are called to fully obey the Lord. Whether others do so or not should not affect our attitude, or our behavior.

Divide and Conquer

November 17

Read Acts 23:6-10; 1 Corinthians 1:10-15

After Paul apologized to the religious tribunal, he gathered his thoughts and began his defense by going on offense. He divided the house by exploiting their theological differences. Paul drove a wedge between the Pharisees and the Sadducees, and they turned on each other. A good old fashioned church fight broke out. It was a sight to behold, and certainly did not gain them any respect from the Roman soldiers who had to rescue Paul from their civil war. The same thing happens today when Christians get ugly and publicly duke it out over their differences. When we drop the cross and take up verbal swords against one another, the dispute over who's right or wrong can drown out the gospel. Jesus gets a black eye when our particular cause becomes more important than the cause of Christ. It's hard for the world to see God's love when His church is busy taking swings at one another.

Courageous Trust

November 18

Read Acts 23:11; Psa. 23:4-5; Deut. 31:6

After his rescue from the mob, Paul received a heavenly visitor. Perhaps Paul's confidence had begun to fade. The Lord came to him, offering encouragement and reassurance that God was still in charge. Even the bravest people will tell you that they have been afraid, and that fear can invade in the blink of an eye. But fear is not the same as cowardice. Fear can often help us excel. Cowardice is fear on steroids -- fear that has mutated and become a cancer in our hearts. When fear invades, who we listen to becomes very important. If we listen to God, courage can grow again. If we listen to the spirit of darkness, cowardice will likely prevail. Paul listened to God. He would never be a free man again. He would remain in chains until his death in Rome. But he lived courageously, and changed the world as a prisoner for Christ. Listen to the Lord. He is with you. Be strong and courageous.

Starving For Vigilante Justice

November 19

Read Acts 23:12-35

Once again the forces of evil hatched a plot to take Paul's life. Forty religious men vowed not to eat again until Paul was killed. If they kept their vow, they starved to death, because God had different plans for Paul. Word of the plot got to Paul, and then to the Roman commander. The Roman commander ordered that Paul be taken to Caesarea under the protection of four hundred seventy soldiers. What we have here is the end game of sin. Like our ancestor Cain, if someone angers us, or we do not get our way, we often connive to hurt them. We plot the demise of those we despise, and in so doing we leave the influence of Christ and come under the influence of the evil one. We may not do them physical harm, but we can wound them deeply with gossip and slander. Brothers and sisters, this should not be. This is not the way of a Christ follower. Repent, before you starve.

Found To Be A Troublemaker

November 20

Read Acts 24:1-9; 1 Corinthians 9:19-23

Paul was taken before Felix, where the high priest Ananias and a lawyer named Tertullus brought charges against him. They started by kissing up to Felix and telling him what a great, insightful ruler he was. Then they began to accuse Paul, saying that he was a troublemaker who stirred up riots and who tried to desecrate the temple. They said he was the ringleader of a "Nazarene sect". Things haven't changed much. Today Paul would likely be dubbed the leader of a "radical fringe group". We can still be labeled as a troublemaker if we zealously proclaim Christ and His gospel. We can be marginalized when we extol the absolute truth and authority of Scripture. Proclaim it anyway! They may label us "kooks" and "radicals", but we have the words of life, and if we speak them and live them, some will be saved! Someday, even if it's on the other side of eternity, someone will thank you.

A Follower of the Way

November 21

Read Acts 24:10-21; Acts 9:1-2; John 14:6

The "Way" was one of the first names given to the early church -- those disciples who believed in the resurrection of Jesus and who followed the risen Lord. Paul had come full circle on his thinking about the Way. Before his meeting with the risen Christ on the road to Damascus, he was a persecutor of those who belonged to the Way. He hunted down those who followed the Way, and had them thrown into prison. But today, we hear him declaring publicly that he has become a follower of the Way. His mind has changed. His heart now belongs to the Christ he once persecuted. His conscience is clear. He denies the charges against him and tells Felix that he is really on trial for believing and preaching the resurrection. Today, we who believe in the resurrection declare that Jesus is the Way -- the way to God and the way to eternal life. Are you a follower of the Way?

Convenient Christianity

November 22

Read Acts 24:22-25; Luke 9:22-26

Paul didn't just make a defense before Felix -- he preached Jesus, and Felix wilted as the fear of God came over him. God had told Paul not to be afraid, and that he would preach the gospel to rulers and emperors. It began with Felix. But Felix put convenience, money, power, and politics ahead of the Lord Jesus. He heard the truth, but it wasn't convenient for him to accept it. It's an age old problem that people still deal with today. Don't wait for the gospel to be convenient. A cross is never convenient. This one cuts both ways. Those who have believed the gospel must be willing to be inconvenienced in order to be His witnesses. Paul was certainly inconvenienced by the gospel. The gospel is also inconvenient for those who hear it. Like Felix, many will fear it and reject it. They don't want to change. Christianity was never meant to be convenient. Stop trying to make it that way.

Paul's Ace in the Hole

November 23

Read Acts 25:1-12; Heb. 10:23; Psa. 145:13-14

Because of Paul's courage in preaching the gospel, he faced continual persecution. At times it must have felt as though God had abandoned him, but Paul was actually right in the center of God's will. Jesus had told him not to fear -- he would present the gospel before kings and emperors. This helped Paul to stand tall and not back away from the truth that the risen Christ was God incarnate. But Paul became weary of the religious zealots of Jerusalem. They were no longer seeking truth -- they were just seeking to snuff out Paul's voice. And if they couldn't do it through legal means, they would do it through hired hit men. So Paul played his ace in the hole. As a Roman citizen he had the right to appeal to Caesar and so he did. Christ's words to him would be fulfilled -- he would stand before emperors and kings. Take heart! In His time, God's words will also be fulfilled in your life.

Promises of Privilege and Pain

November 24

Read Acts 25:13-22; Acts 9:15-16

Festus confessed that he didn't understand why the Jews wanted to kill Paul, whose only offense was claiming that a dead man named Jesus was still alive. Festus joins a long list of politicians with no spiritual compass who must confess that spiritual truth is above their pay grade. God had promised Paul that he would carry Christ's name before kings and suffer for it. God keeps His promises. Paul appeared before King Agrippa. The Lord will also keep His promises to us -- promises that include both privilege and pain. When we bear witness about a dead man named Jesus who is still alive, we will receive blessing and endure suffering. For the Christian, it always comes back to Christ's resurrection. Our faith rises or falls on its truth. If it happened with Jesus, it will happen with us, and death need not be feared -- even if we stand before lost, indifferent, and hostile kings.

What's Wrong With This Picture?

November 25

Read Acts 26:1-8; Acts 23:6-9; John 5:39-40

Paul was glad to appear before King Agrippa because Agrippa knew more about Jewish thinking than Felix or Festus. Thus Paul knew that the king would understand when he spoke about the hope of the Pharisees. They believed in an afterlife -- a resurrection of the dead. Paul told King Agrippa that it was because of his hope in the resurrection that he was on trial, and wondered out loud why they would put him on trial for holding to the same hope that they did. Why would the Pharisees consider it incredible that God would raise Jesus from the dead, when they were already on record as advocates for the resurrection of the dead? Paul was asking, "What's wrong with this picture?" We could ask the same question today. Why would so many who believe in an afterlife, refuse to come to Christ, who rose from the dead and promises eternal life? What's wrong with this picture?

Turning Points

November 26

Read Acts 26:9-15; Philippians 3:2-7

Paul told Agrippa that he once was a very zealous Pharisee who opposed the name of Jesus. He persecuted the church with all his energy. He even blessed the killing of Christians. He had been obsessed with the destruction of the church, traveling far and wide to hunt down converts to Christ. He tried to force them to recant their faith, and to publicly disown Jesus. But there came a turning point -- a day when his heart changed. Paul met the risen Christ face to face. This Jesus that Paul thought was dead appeared to him on the Damascus road and spoke to him -- a difficult task for a dead man. Paul came to a fork in the road and chose the Jesus way. He chose to believe his eyes and ears and heart. He chose faith. We all have a turning point -- a time and place where our hearts have the opportunity to turn to Jesus. Where was your turning point? Don't turn back!

Appointed for Service

November 27

Read Acts 26:16; John 15:16; 1 Timothy 2:7

Jesus flattened Paul on the Damascus Road, but also appointed him to some specific tasks. Paul received a new assignment for his new life. First, he was to get back on his feet. God does not save us to keep us down, and it's hard to serve God unless we are standing in faith. Jesus then appointed Paul to His service. The gospel is about more than forgiveness of sin. It's also about calling. Paul was appointed as a servant and a witness. Servants have a master, and do that master's will. They give more than they receive. Witnesses don't talk about themselves, but testify to what someone else has done. Paul was appointed to testify about what he had seen and what he would be shown. Christians, our task is the same. We are called to stand up and witness to what Christ has done -- and what He will do as our faith witness grows and deepens. We have been appointed for service by God.

The Mission

November 28

Read Acts 26:17-18; John 3:20-21; Isa. 42:6-7

Paul was given a new purpose in life by the risen Jesus. He was rescued, and then sent to become a change agent in the lives of both the Jews and the Gentiles. His mission would be to bring sight to those who were spiritually blind. Through his preaching, many would come out of darkness and begin to walk in the light of Christ. Jesus would give them new eyes, and they would begin to see life differently. Many would turn away from the prince of darkness and begin to follow the Light of the world. The power of Satan would dwindle in their lives, as the power of God grew. Our mission today is the same as Paul's. With the mercy and forgiveness of God comes a changed life -- a new life. Like Paul, we are called to bring light to those who are blind, and to free those who are captives of darkness. We do that by bringing them to Jesus. He is the Light. Lift up His name. Let His light shine!

Forgiveness and Sanctification

November 29

Read Acts 26:17-18; Romans 15:15-16; 2 Thessalonians 2:13-14

Every soul needs forgiveness and sanctification in order to enter into eternity with the Lord. We need a pardon from our sin (forgiveness), and we need to be made holy (sanctification). God is holy, and His coming Kingdom will be holy. No sin or darkness will be found there. Jesus sent Paul to preach this truth among the Gentiles so they could "receive forgiveness of sins and a place among those who are sanctified by faith." We have all sinned and need God's forgiveness to receive a place with Him. Jesus is the way. On the cross, He paid the price for our pardon. We all need to be made holy. Jesus is the way. When we put our faith in Him, we are sanctified by the Holy Spirit. We all need forgiveness and sanctification to enter eternity with God. This is what Paul and Christ's disciples taught, and it is what true Christ followers will be teaching today.

Gospel of Obedience

November 30

Read Acts 26:19-20; Matt. 3:8; James 2:14-26

Hearing God's call is great, but if we do not answer that call, we live in disobedience to the Lord. Paul was not disobedient. He answered God's call, and began to preach the gospel. And now, as Paul stood before King Agrippa, he witnessed to the changes the risen Jesus had made in his life, and he shared the gospel in a single sentence -- repent, turn to God, and prove your repentance by your deeds. Repentance means we believe God about the gravity of our sins, and in our sorrow, we become willing to change our direction in life. We turn away from sin and turn toward the Lord. We leave our old life for a new life in Christ. Our repentance is then proven by the way we live out this new life. Salvation is by grace through faith, but if it does not change us, it is not God's salvation. Repentance is life changing. Our lives will bear its fruit. Our deeds will back up our faith story.

God's Script

December 1

Read Acts 26:19-22; Acts 4:23-30

Paul declared his obedience to the Lord and his complete dependence upon God's plan. Even though he was a prisoner, he wanted everyone to know that Jesus was alive and was with him as he shared the gospel with King Agrippa. Paul let Agrippa know that God was in charge, for God had written the script. The coming, the suffering, the death, and the resurrection of Christ were all the fulfillment of prophecies written into the script centuries before they happened. Paul's appearance before the king was also no accident -- his life was in God's hands, not Agrippa's. Paul told Agrippa that the resurrection was God's plan for everyone. King Agrippa was now face to face with the Truth. He would never be able to stand in front of God and say, "I didn't know about Jesus." He had been evangelized. God has written a script for you too. Will you speak it? Will you live it out?

Interruption and Condescension

December 2

Read Acts 26:24; Acts 26:28

When Paul shared the truth about Jesus, the response of Festus and King Agrippa was typical. It is the age-old strategy of "interruption and condescension". Paul's preaching struck a nerve, so Festus interrupted him, accused him of being insane, and labeled him as a "wacky fundamentalist". King Agrippa told Paul that he was not gullible enough to become a Christian. These are elitist responses. Festus and Agrippa were doing what powerful men have done for centuries -- if you can't argue with the message, discredit the messenger. They were smug and condescending to a chosen apostle of God, but inside, their hearts were trembling. They labeled Paul, but they knew they had heard something significant. Many of those we share the gospel with today will employ a similar strategy. Don't be surprised or discouraged. We know the Way, the Truth, and the Life. Speak with confidence.

The Insanity of Unbelief

December 3

Read Acts 26:25-27; 2 Thess. 2:9-13

Paul told Festus and Agrippa that he was not insane, and that with all the available public knowledge of the resurrection, it was actually unbelief that constituted insanity. Hundreds had seen the risen Christ. The church was growing by leaps and bounds because it was based in truth, not insanity. God's offer of grace and eternity was available, even to Festus and Agrippa. But to accept it, they would have to cast off all pride, stop worrying about what others might think, and believe the words Paul had spoken about Jesus. One would have to be crazy to pass up a deal like this, but that's what Festus and Agrippa did. Their minds had slipped into the insanity of unbelief. Not that much has changed. Like Paul, we share a gospel that is reasonable and true, but often we are labeled as ignorant, gullible, and insane. The insanity of unbelief is alive and well in our culture today.

The Prayer for Unbelief

December 4

Read Acts 26:28-29; John 17:13-21; Eph. 3:10-19

Paul didn't berate King Agrippa -- he just spoke the truth to him. Paul's prayer for the king and his court was that they would become like him, except for his chains. He prayed that they would all come to faith in Jesus, and declared himself a worthy model for others to follow. This was just too much for the King and the Governor, and they brought the hearing to an end, never realizing that one day they would bow before the Christ that Paul was proclaiming. Every knee will bow! And just like them, many will flee when confronted by a confident Christian preaching the truth of the gospel. They will live out their lives without Christ, and die lost. But we keep preaching, because some will be saved. Could you make the claim Paul made? Could you say, "I pray that you will become what I am."? This was not conceit. This was confidence in Christ. Would others benefit if they emulated your faith?

The Flight of Unbelief

December 5

Read Acts 26:30-32; Acts 7:51-58

Two things happened when Paul began speaking about the risen Christ. First, the king and the governor heard more than they wanted to hear, and left the room. Second, they avoided discussing Jesus. They spoke about legality rather than spirituality. They discussed what to do with Paul, rather than what to do with Jesus. They focused on the things of this world rather than the call of eternity. When the unbelieving world hears the name of Jesus, they often go into avoidance mode. If putting us down or shouting us down doesn't work, they clamor to change the subject. They resort to making a lot of noise, covering their ears, and closing their eyes. You could call it "the flight of unbelief". There is power in the name of Jesus -- power that threatens the status quo. We cannot control what others do with the name of Jesus, but we can control what we do with it. Lift up His name!

Against the Wind

December 6

Read Acts 27:1-9

It is difficult to sail or run against the wind and make good time. Back in the 1970's, there was a hit song that advised, "You don't spit into the wind." The reason should be obvious. As Paul was being taken to Rome by ship, the winds continuously blew against them, and they ended up in places where they hadn't intended to go. They wasted much time sailing sideways. There is a lesson here. We should exercise caution when the winds of God blow against us. If we are not careful, we can squander our life running against the wind. If we try to do everything under our own power, we can end up in places where we didn't intend to be. Maybe it's time to move with the winds of God instead of against them. There may be times when we are called to run against the wind, but if the wind is constantly blowing against us, perhaps we should consider a change of course. Stop spitting into the wind!

Fickle Winds

December 7

Read Acts 27:9-17; Proverbs 3:5-6

Paul warned against going to sea, but the ship's crew ignored his prophetic words and decided to sail on. When a favorable south wind came, they set sail, but it wasn't long before they were struggling to remain afloat in a hurricane-force gale. The winds of this world are fickle. We can be sailing along just fine, with the wind at our backs, but in a heartbeat the wind can change, and we find ourselves in the middle of a storm that forces us off course and threatens to sink us. God's word often warns us against following the world's fickle winds, but we think we know better. The Lord calls us not to go here or there, but we ignore His word and head out on our own without His blessing. God tells us to wait for His timing, but we charge ahead. Our disobedience will always lead us out into dangerous waters, where the winds of this world are fickle. Life goes better when we trust and obey God's word.

The Up Side to Storms

December 8

Read Acts 27:18-19; Phil. 3:8-9; 2 Cor. 12:9

The storm battering Paul's ship forced the crew to make some desperate decisions. The possibility of sinking was very real and there was only one option left -- lighten the ship so it could ride higher in the water. To this end they began to throw cargo and tackle overboard. Cargo becomes meaningless when your destination is the bottom of the sea. Everything non-essential went into the raging waters. When the storms of life come, we are often forced to prioritize. When hard pressed, we must take a hard look at what we consider to be the "essentials". We must make some decisions about what can stay and what must go. This can be difficult, but it will also be extremely beneficial. Ridding our lives of extra baggage can be freeing. We can establish new boundaries and new priorities. If we refuse to do this, we may sink and perish. Storms force us to prioritize, and that's not all bad.

Hope and Despair

December 9

Read Acts 27:20-25; Rom. 15:13; 2 Cor. 1:8-11

Storms can drive us to despair. When a storm drags on and on, it can wear us down, drain us of our will, and discourage us to the point of giving up. The storm that battered Paul's ship had gone on for fourteen days. It had come to the point where they had given up all hope for survival. But despair is about mindset more than reality. It is based in feelings more than facts. The antidote for despair is encouragement and hope. This is what Paul offered the passengers and crew as he gave glory to God. He declared that by the grace of God, all of them would survive. The Lord had spoken words of assurance to Paul and he believed God. In a time of calamity and despair, Paul the prisoner rose to spiritual leadership. He became the voice of God as he spoke words of hope and encouragement into those around him. This is still our calling as Christians. Jesus saves!

Discomforting Prophecy

December 10

Read Acts 27:26; Isaiah 30:10; Matt. 5:45b

After encouraging the passengers and crew, Paul shared a second prophetic word -- the ship would run aground on an island. These words were discomforting, as running aground and surviving a storm at sea do not usually go together. But Paul spoke what the Spirit had shown him. Everyone goes through storms in life, and the truth is, they always cost us something. Storms come for both the obedient and the disobedient. There were both carnal men and godly men aboard Paul's ship -- both sinners and the surrendered. They all went through the same storm. No one is immune to storms. Paul had done God's will at every step of the way since his conversion, yet he suffered through the storm along with those who had been disobedient. So the question is not, "Will storms come?" but rather, "Will our faith hold up when we are going through them?"

Storm Damage

December 11

Read Acts 27:27-29; Jonah 1:1-6; Psa. 62:5-8

Paul's ship had been battered by a storm for fourteen days when the crew sensed that something was changing, and discovered they were approaching land. This was not good news. In the darkness of night, they were in danger of running aground or striking a barrier reef, which would likely cause the ship to break apart. Death seemed imminent. As a last resort, they dropped anchors to hold them in place and prayed for daylight. If they could see, they might be able to navigate through the reefs, get safely to shore, and avert a disaster. There are times when the storms of life seem to dwarf us and swallow us up. The results of a storm can be disastrous for us and those around us. When we are engulfed in a storm, sometimes all that we can do is drop anchor, try to hold steady, and pray for light to come. Jesus is our anchor. Jesus is our light. Trust Him in times of storms.

Stay Onboard

December 12

Read Acts 27:30-32; John 3:3-7; John 15:4-6

Big ships need deep water, but lifeboats can skim over rocky reefs. That's why some of the sailors on Paul's ship tried to lower a lifeboat in order to save themselves. You find out who your friends are in a storm. Paul saw what the sailors were doing and told the Roman soldiers that they could not be saved unless the sailors stayed aboard. The soldiers believed Paul and cut the ropes holding the lifeboat. You also find out who truly believes when the storms of life come. The soldiers could have used the lifeboat to save themselves, but they cut the ropes because they had seen enough of Paul to know that he was no ordinary prisoner. He was a man of God and they put their faith in his words and his God. There are many places in Scripture where God says, "Unless you do this, you cannot be saved." We would be wise to do what God says and stay onboard His ship.

Strength to Endure

December 13

Read Acts 27:33-40; Romans 15:4-6

The crew knew they were approaching land, and developed a risky plan for survival. When your ship is sinking, you must think outside the box. Safe and traditional planning can be a ticket to the bottom of the sea. In a desperate attempt to make land, the crew threw their food supply overboard to lighten the ship, cut all their anchors loose, raised the sails, and drove full speed ahead for shore. Surviving a storm also requires strength and endurance, and Paul encouraged everyone to eat something before they gambled on this one last chance at survival. But Paul also fed everyone with encouragement. He gave public thanks to his God in the midst of the storm and prophesied that not one of them would be lost at sea. They would all survive. Christians, when going through a storm, do not shrink from the risks, and feed on God's word for strength to endure. Trust in the Lord!

The Best Laid Plans

December 14

***Read Acts 27:41-44; Psalm 33:10-11;
Proverbs 16:9; Proverbs 19:21***

Even man's best laid plans can fail in the storms
of life. As Paul's ship made a desperate dash for
shore, it hit a sandbar and began to break up.
Not only was there the danger of drowning, the
soldiers were going to kill Paul and the other
prisoners to prevent them from escaping. But
Paul had won favor with the centurion, and he
ordered the soldiers to stand down. This one
Roman soldier changed history. By God's grace,
he protected the man who would write much of
the New Testament. Leadership matters,
especially in times of great storms. Today, it is
not God's will that anyone should perish, but that
all would come to repentance and new life. If the
storms of life are breaking your ship apart, grab
hold of Jesus and head for shore. You need not
perish in the deep waters of sorrow or by the
sharp sword of sin. Trust in God's plan.

Grace and Salvation

December 15

Read Acts 27:44; 2 Cor. 12:9; Eph. 2:4-5

After despairing of life for fourteen stormy days and nights… after thwarting an attempt by cowards to save themselves… after Paul and the other prisoners were spared from being killed… and after the ship ran aground and was battered to pieces in a failed attempt to reach the shore… the hand of God reached down and saved everyone on board. Not a single person was lost. This was no accident! Nor was it luck or fate! This was the grace of God. This is what happens when people follow godly leadership and trust in God's mercy. We endure the storms of life by God's grace, and survive the ultimate storm of death by faith in His grace. Trusting Jesus won't prevent us from going through storms, but it gives us guidance and comfort as we endure them, and His grace delivers us safely to that eternal shore when our time comes. Jesus saves by grace, through faith.

Offering Hospitality

December 16

Read Acts 28:1-2; Romans 12:13; 1 Peter 4:9

As those on the ship struggled ashore, the people there were very friendly and showed "unusual kindness". Hospitality is a trait found in most cultures. There are millions of nice people in this world who do not know the Lord. Many of them outshine Christians in kindness and generosity. But we must not mistake kindness for being right with God. We must never forget that even the kindest of people can still be sinners in need of a Savior. Nice people need Jesus too. All Christians are called on to be hospitable, but not all are obedient to this call. Many who would consider themselves to be "doctrinally astute" could also be classified as "hospitality deficient". This should not be. One can be hospitable without being a Christian, but one cannot be an obedient Christian and be inhospitable. Kindness is a fruit of the Spirit, and the term "Unkind Christian" is an oxymoron.

Bad Things Happen to Good People

December 17

Read Acts 28:3-4; Ecclesiastes 9:11-12

As Paul continued to serve by gathering firewood, a poisonous viper latched onto his hand. Since Paul survived the storm, only to be bitten by a viper, the islanders believed that he must be a bad man who was cursed by the gods. But the God of Scripture had something else in mind. They were about to see a miracle as great as surviving the storm. You cannot judge someone's faith by their circumstances. You cannot always tie someone's physical condition to their spiritual condition. Sometimes they are connected, sometimes they are not. Bad things happen to good people. There is no scientific formula in this area. There are no pat answers. So Christians, let's stop offering pat answers. Let's cease and desist from making pious pronouncements or judgments when people go through hard times. Loving those who suffer in this life is the Jesus way.

The Fickleness of Fate

December 18

Read Acts 28:4-6; Acts 14:8-15

The islanders of Malta believed that Paul had been cursed by the goddess of Justice, because after surviving a violent storm and shipwreck, he was almost immediately bitten by a viper. Their fate based gods would never let something like this happen to a good person. But the gods of fate are fickle, even though many today still worship these gods. To complicate matters, the God of Scripture threw a wrench in the works -- instead of dying, Paul shook the viper off, and went about his business unharmed. The local gurus were then forced to change their narrative, and make Paul into a god. If the viper did not harm him, he must have divine power. This time they were at least partly right. Paul was not a god, but he did possess divine power, and he would use that power to change the way an entire island thought about the God of Creation. This is also our calling as Christians.

Redeeming the Time

December 19

Read Acts 28:7-10; Matt. 5:16; Eph. 5:15-16

Paul spent three months on Malta, and he redeemed the time wisely. He had learned to make the most of every opportunity and to let his light shine wherever he went. He was invited to visit Publius, the governor of the island, and he stayed there three days. While he was there, he healed the governor's father, and "the rest of the sick on the island" were brought to him. As was his habit, Paul certainly gave glory to God and preached Jesus while he was there, so one could say that the very inconvenient shipwreck, as well as the poisonous snake bite, led to an entire island being evangelized. This is what it means to redeem the times. As Christians, we are called to be agents of change wherever we go. We are to take the healing, transforming power of Christ into every situation. Stop whining and give glory to God. Lift up the name of Jesus, especially in life's difficult days.

A Ship of Irony

December 20

Read Acts 28:11; Mark 10:45; Rom. 5:8; 1 Jn. 3:16

Paul's ship on the final leg of his journey to Rome was dedicated to Castor and Pollux. Castor and Pollux were mythical twin sons who shared the same mother, but had different fathers. Pollux was immortal because his father was Zeus, the god of the universe, ruler of the heavens and the earth, and father of all gods and men. Castor on the other hand, had a human father and was mortal. The two were very close, and when Castor died, Pollux asked Zeus to let him share his immortality with Castor. The twins were then transformed into the heavenly constellation of Gemini. It is ironic that the very human Paul, who would eventually die for preaching about eternal life in the divine Christ, would be transported on a ship dedicated to the concept of one who is immortal, laying down his life for one who is not. Jesus came to lay down His life for us. Merry Christmas!

And So We Came to Rome

December 21

Read Acts 28:12-14; Gal. 4:4-5; Heb. 3:14

Things that appear insignificant have a way of becoming momentous events. Luke says today, "And so we came to Rome." Consider the weight of those words and the event they describe. The gospel, born in the tiny backwater town of Bethlehem, had now arrived in mighty Rome. Paul was bringing Jesus, the King of Kings, to meet Caesar, who thought he was the king of all kings. Paul, thought to be a prisoner of Rome, was coming to town as the evangelist of Rome. Paul arrives in Rome -- the end of the road for him, the place where he would die -- and Luke writes matter-of-factly, "And so we came to Rome." Eventually, we all come to the last stop on our journey. We are all on a road that will end up in a "Rome" of some kind. Are you ready for that? Will you finish with the same assurance with which you started? Will you speak the truth even unto death? Lord, help us all to finish well.

People Matter

December 22

Read Acts 28:15: Romans 12:10-18

At a junction of highways about twelve miles outside of Rome, Paul and his escort were met by some Christians from Rome who had come out to greet him. It was a hero's welcome. When it comes to priorities, loving God and loving people should be at the top of our list. Jerusalem was into religion, Rome was into power, but Paul was into people. Those who came out to greet Paul were some of the greatest tributes a man could have. These people, not his religious accomplishments, encouraged Paul the most. They became his testimony, and his eulogy. So let us remember that in the end, it is people who matter most… not status, or fame, or money, or career… not where you live, or what you drive, or what honors you receive. As we approach the end of our lives, people will matter more than anything except Jesus. Where are you investing your time and energy today?

The Hope of Israel

December 23

Read Acts 28:16-22; Jeremiah 17:13-14

Paul called the Jewish leaders of Rome together to explain why he had come there in custody. Those leaders had already heard many people denigrating this "sect" called Christianity. Their negativity did not deter Paul. The Jews in Rome were treated to the zeal of a born again believer, as Paul spoke fearlessly about Jesus, "the hope of Israel". The gospel that got him arrested and sent to Rome was the same gospel that he preached when he got there. His message did not change. This is still our message Christians! Jesus Christ, born of a virgin in Bethlehem, and crucified in Jerusalem for our sins, is still "the hope of Israel", and of the entire world. Jeremiah declares that "the hope of Israel" comes as a "spring of living water", to heal us and to save us. "Joy to the world the Lord is come. Let Earth receive her King. Let every heart prepare Him room." Merry Christmas!

From Morning Till Evening

December 24

Read Acts 28:23; 1 Cor. 9:16; 2 Thess. 3:13

If an honor roll of tireless preachers were compiled, Paul's name would be at the top of the list. Even as a prisoner confined to his quarters, he continued to preach. If anyone had an excuse to succumb to self-pity, it was Paul. But he persisted in sharing the gospel with anyone who would listen. Paul was a man on a mission. Even though the verses here in Acts do not spell it out, he seemed to know that his time was short. From dawn to dark, his every waking hour, Paul taught about the Kingdom of our Lord. He tirelessly continued to lead as many as possible to the knowledge of salvation in Christ. His texts were the Prophets and the Law of Moses, for salvation by grace through faith is a timeless theme of Scripture. Christians, in this season of joy, our task is the same -- to tirelessly share the truth about the One born in Bethlehem. Merry Christmas!

Salvation Has Been Sent

December 25

Read Acts 28:24-28; Luke 4:18-19; Matt. 23:37

For the religious Jews of Rome, the objection to Paul's gospel was the same as it had been with the Jews in Jerusalem. They could not buy the idea of a suffering Messiah, and they definitely could not believe in a Savior who would be interested in Gentiles. The majority suffered from hard hearts, deaf ears, and blind eyes. Do not join them in their unbelief. Christ was born in Bethlehem. God came as a baby. The Word became flesh. He came for us all -- male and female, rich and poor, good and bad, Gentile and Jew. The angel said to the shepherds near Bethlehem, "The good and joyous news is that the Christ child, born in a manger, has come for all people." What the angels declared, Paul preached -- Jesus Christ came so that all who believe can be saved. Salvation has been sent. Believe God. Come to Jesus. This was Paul's message. This is the message of Christmas.

Like a Drink Offering

December 26

Read Acts 28:30; 2 Timothy 4:6-8

The book of Acts doesn't end in a tidy way. It leaves us hanging, as if Luke just stopped writing, or a page or two has been torn from the end of the book. We want to hear, "and they all lived happily ever after." But the story of Christ's church has never been about finding happiness. Instead it is about finding salvation, carrying our cross, and following Him in faith and obedience as a disciple. We do not know for sure what happened to Paul, but we do know what happened to the church. It continued to grow in number, miracles continued to happen, and martyrs continued to be produced. Tradition holds that Paul was one of those martyred in Rome -- his life poured out like a drink offering. We may call that unfair, and question God's plan, but every life has a Rome, and Christ calls us to be as faithful in our dying as we have been in our living. Will that be your story?

Boldly and Without Hindrance

December 27

Read Acts 28:31; Acts 4:31; Acts 9:28; Acts 19:8

Paul preached boldly from start to finish. He stood eye to eye with both religious and political powers and did not blink. He boldly proclaimed Jesus as Lord and King in a place where Caesar was hailed as Lord and King. Paul seems brave beyond measure in a day when timid Christians get squeamish if someone even frowns at their faith. Luke says Paul also preached without hindrance. Perhaps Nero thought that people would see the fallacy of this pathetic little religion called Christianity. Nero was mistaken. Many were converted, and since all roads led to Rome, Christ's name traveled back out to the places where those roads originated. It was like putting an airborne virus into the ductwork of a large building. The gospel traveled everywhere. Paul eventually lost his life in Rome, but Rome became an accessory to Christianity by allowing Paul to preach boldly and without hindrance.

Last Things

December 28

Read Acts 28:31; Matt. 10:22; Rev. 2:26

What would you make a priority if you knew you only had a short time left to live? Paul chose to preach the Kingdom and teach about Jesus. God's Kingdom is more important than any earthly kingdom or institution. It is the eternal Kingdom. Nothing should take priority over serving and growing the Kingdom of our Lord. This should affect every aspect of our life in our every remaining moment. There is only one King and one Lord. His name is Jesus. Paul taught that Christ is the Savior who saves and the Lord who leads. He is the gold standard for godly humanity. Our times and our souls are in His hands. In the short time Paul had left, he boldly preached the Kingdom and taught about Jesus. Perhaps this would make an excellent mission statement for the church in these last days. It also makes a great purpose statement for each of us in the time we have left here on this Earth.

The Cost of Truth and Light

December 29

Read 1 Cor. 4:9-13; Heb. 12:1-3; Heb. 13:7

The stories of Stephen, James, John, Barnabas, Peter, and Paul should remind us that declaring God's Kingdom and sharing the truth and light of Christ will often come at a high cost. Paul once wrote that the apostles were condemned, dishonored, homeless, cursed, persecuted, and slandered -- like slaves at the "end of the procession". They were "fools for Christ". They were the "scum of the Earth", and the "refuse of the world". Does this sound like the "prosperity gospel" to you? Yet we are called by the writer of Hebrews to look up to these leaders, and to "imitate their faith". If you have placed your faith in Christ, you are surrounded by a band of celestial heroes who gave their lives to proclaim the truth and light of Jesus Christ. They not only recorded history, they made history. God help us to also be history makers as we live out our faith and share the light and truth of Christ in our day.

Living Beyond Your Means

December 30

Read Acts 3:12; Romans 4:20-21;
1 Corinthians 2:4-5; Ephesians 3:20

One cannot read the book of Acts and not feel God's call to live beyond our means spiritually. The early church did this on a regular basis, and we should grow into it as modern day disciples. When we live beyond our means, God receives glory. The apostles often reminded people that it was God's power, not theirs, that accomplished the impossible. They always pointed people to the power of the resurrected Christ. They were living beyond their means. Abraham was one of the first to do so. He did not waver in faith even though he waited on God's promise for many years. Living beyond your means is about faith. It's about knowing that all things are possible with God. It's about trusting God, even when things look dark, and prayers go unanswered. This is how the early disciples lived and died. Will you do the same? Live beyond your means!

Not in Vain

December 31

Read Acts 26:20; 2 Tim. 4:2-5; 1 Cor. 15:54-58

Paul knew that death was imminent, but he lived fearlessly. Death has no hold on those who truly belong to Jesus. We are but a vapor -- our immortal souls confined for a time in mortal bodies. From dust we came and to dust we will return. But we were created for eternity, and to really live beyond our means, we must become convinced that we are working for a crown that can never be received here on Earth. We must abandon the fear of death and live as though we were applying for a position in eternity. We must repent, turn to God, and begin a relationship with the Lord Jesus Christ. Christianity is not just a philosophy that we believe in as we pass through life -- it is life itself. It is not a consumer product that we try for a while to see if it works -- it consumes us as it works in us. Keep the faith. Finish the race. Spend the rest of your life living beyond your means. Your labor is not in vain.